R.E.M.

BY PETER HOGAN

Copyright © 1995 Omnibus Press (A Division of Book Sales Limited)

Edited by Johnny Rogan & Chris Charlesworth
Cover & Book designed by 4i, London
Picture research by Nikki Russell

ISBN: 0.7119.4901.8 Order No.OP47769

Exclusive Distributors:
Book Sales Limited, 8/9 Frith Street, London W1V 5TZ, UK.
Music Sales Corporation, 257 Park Avenue South, New York, NY 10010, USA.
Music Sales Pty Limited, 120 Rothschild Avenue, Rosebery, NSW 2018, Australia.

To the Music Trade only:
Music Sales Limited, 8/9, Frith Street, London W1V 5TZ, UK.

Photo credits: Front cover, LFI. All other pictures supplied by LFI, Retna & Barrie Plummer.
Every effort has been made to trace the copyright holders of the photographs
in this book but one or two were unreachable. We would be grateful if the photographers
concerned would contact us.

Printed in the United Kingdom by Ebenezer Baylis & Son, Worcester.

A catalogue record for this book is available from the British Library.

OMNIBUS PRESS
LONDON · NEW YORK · SYDNEY

CONTENTS

INTRODUCTION..V

MURMUR...1
RECKONING/FILE UNDER WATER 11
FABLES OF THE RECONSTRUCTION/
RECONSTRUCTION OF THE FABLES 19
LIFES RICH PAGEANT 29
DEAD LETTER OFFICE 37
DOCUMENT 45
GREEN 55
OUT OF TIME...63
AUTOMATIC FOR THE PEOPLE 73
MONSTER 83

COMPILATION ALBUMS 93
ANY FINALLY..102
VIDEOS 105

INDEX 112

Introduction

ONE: RANDOM ENGLISH MEMORIES

Milton Keynes Concert Bowl, June 22, 1985: I'm up above the stage, hanging off scaffolding in a gale force wind, the rain stinging my face like needles. The reason I'm risking my neck like this is simply so that I can get a decent view of R.E.M. playing live a few yards below me.

But it's pissing down, literally. Not only have the heavens opened, but the bored festival crowd – impatient to see headliners U2 – are giving all the support bands a really hard time. Those down at the front have been drinking beer out of big plastic bottles, which they've filled with urine and are throwing on stage at any band they dislike – which includes R.E.M. (And this is not even vaguely funny – *Melody Maker* photographer Andy Catlin gets hit on the head by one of these things, and spends the rest of the day semi-concussed.)

Peter Buck manages to skip nimbly over the rolling bottles, barely missing a note. But Michael Stipe is vulnerable, rooted to his mike stand. "Oh, thank you *so* much," he tells the crowd after one near-miss. "This is not what summer's like in Georgia *at all!*"

They do their best, but the crowd aren't much interested in listening to them, especially since the set is taken almost exclusively from their new album (which hardly anyone has heard yet); the gig is scarcely what you'd call a success. Backstage an hour later, I go to knock on their trailer door to commiserate, but am headed off at the pass by their tour manager Geoff Trump. "I wouldn't," he says glumly.

The reason I am hanging around with R.E.M. is because I am, at this point, their English press officer. I'd had the job for a month or so, having been brought on board by IRS to help promote the new album, 'Fables Of The Reconstruction'. It is an easy job. Not only do I like R.E.M.'s music, including this new album, but so do the English music press, who are eager to provide coverage (especially when this means they get a free trip to Georgia). Good interviews are done, front covers are promised (and delivered), the reviews are all a press officer could hope for.

And then R.E.M. fly into Britain for the Milton Keynes gig, followed by a handful of small club dates. And they are not in good shape. They're roadweary, and have been for years; and this time they're touring to support an album they feel at best ambivalent about. They'd had a rotten time recording it in London, and now they're back and the city itself is reminding them of that experience. This was the year of Michael Stipe's frequent mad haircut changes (a reflection of the inner turmoil), and he has enough problems without talking to the press any more; quite sensibly, he has decided he's not going to do so, and will leave the media chores to Peter Buck and Mike Mills while he goes cruising art galleries and shopping.

This would be fine if he wasn't the one everybody wants to talk to, but there's no way he'll budge, and I respect that (eventually Peter lures him out, to talk to *NME* late one night in my Newcastle hotel room). Peter and Mike grin and bear it (ace chaps that they prove to be), which means that I get to have animated conversations about music with Peter while rifling through the suitcase of cassettes he's dragged along for a mobile soundtrack. Mike, meanwhile, pumps me with questions about all things English. But Bill Berry grins even more than they do, since he doesn't have to bear any of it (drummers tend to come pretty low on the rock-journalist hit list) and knows he's going to be left in peace. My abiding memory of Bill is that grin (often accompanied by a wink, and the kind of mugging he does in the 'Shiny Happy People' video) and those wolfish eyebrows, frequently seen over the top of a beer bottle.

But if the critics loved R.E.M., the public still barely knew they existed. The club dates I witnessed seldom had more than a hundred people in the audience, but R.E.M. were *terrific* live – all the more amazing given how roadragged they were. The sight of Michael Stipe singing his heart out on 'Driver 8', hanging onto the mike stand for dear life in a half-empty (and grotty) Newcastle disco is one I won't easily forget.

They were shunted round the country in a tiny van (just the four of them and Geoff), without much sleep or decent food. They barely had time to change clothes, and often looked like they'd slept in them (Peter Buck has a fund of tips about survival on the road, most of them to do with maintaining minimal cleanliness levels). And there was no end to it. I remember asking Mike when he expected to see his home in Athens again, and he brightened considerably at just the thought of a few days off for Thanksgiving in November, five months further down the road.

Throughout all of this, they suffered journalists, fans and the occasional fool; I doubt if they did it gladly, but they were *always* polite and even-tempered: true Southern gentlemen, in fact. You ask me, whatever success they've attained since then, they've well and truly earned it ten times over.

TWO: REASON EQUALS MOTIVE

"The secret of R.E.M. is that Mike doesn't play bass like a bass player, Peter doesn't play guitar like a guitar player, and I don't sing like a singer. And Bill just sort of holds it all together." – Michael Stipe, 1990.

"R.E.M. is part lies, part heart, part truth and part garbage." – Peter Buck, 1988.

In the early Eighties, while new British groups were toying with techno and a flock of haircuts, more style than substance, the last, best hope of rock music seemed to lie in America. There a synthesis of the best aspects of both punk and hippie was taking place: the groups The Three O'Clock's Michael Quercio dubbed the Paisley Underground. Dream Syndicate, Green On Red, The Bangs, The Long Ryders... dozens of 'em, mostly guitar-based with at least one eye fixed on the Sixties.

And then there were R.E.M., who were different. Why have they been so successful? Because they were fronted by someone who appeared to be a general purpose art-rock weirdo in the David Byrne mould, which made them a gift to the media, for a kick-off. And because – more than those other groups – R.E.M. seemed to be offering something original: *new* psychedelia, if you like. As a result they became, in the words of Peter Buck, "the acceptable face of the unacceptable". Or perhaps they were acceptable because nobody really knew what they *were*. But Stipe's eccentric approach was married to the others' solid musicianship (and even Stipe had been in a covers band – Bad Habits – back in East St. Louis). Not that R.E.M. were (or are) Michael's backing band, a mistake many seem to have trouble getting out of their heads.

They grew up in private, and matured their craft among friends. They came from the South, from Athens, Georgia – a university town that had already given the world The B-52's. It had a party scene, rather than clubs, and was boho/arty rather then faddishly fashionable. Though they came from a healthy local music scene (Pylon, Love Tractor, The Side Effects, all appeared about the same time), none of the other bands really transcended Athens' town boundaries.

One reason why R.E.M. did has to lie with the lyrics, more akin to poetry than any in rock to date. Michael Stipe told *Musician* magazine in 1985: "The first thing for me is building those walls, coming up with rules – with these turns of phrase – and using them differently, changing them so that old rule doesn't apply anymore and a new rule has taken its place."

Analysing his songwriting ten years later, Michael Stipe confessed: "I was a bad lyricist. I wrote stream of consciousness. Stream of consciousness doesn't make sense. It does on some level, on some very emotional level, but I've always said that R.E.M. is emotional. The impact of the band and the sound of the voice and the music is like a visual landscape. It's not something you can put on a table and mathematically tear apart and have it make sense." Continuing, he advised listeners: "Don't dissect us in a classical, linear way; come at it from somewhere else."

And their audience did, delighted at the challenge and relieved at the change from pop pap. R.E.M. didn't sing about love much (till recently); they sang about childhood, history, time and memory, animals, the South and God only knew what else. It made a nice change.

And the bottom line is : R.E.M. are very talented, *and* (then as now) in tune with their times. (Don Gehman: "They're very good at reinventing themselves. They stay current because they're always looking to find new ground to cover.")

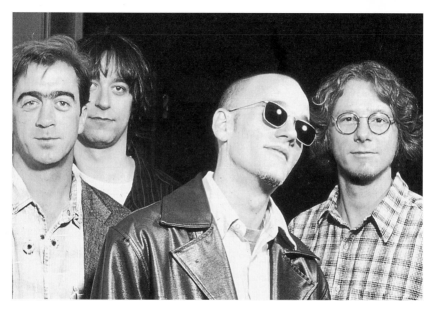

Also (as we have seen), they work bloody hard. They've reached the top while managing to avoid most of the pitfalls of stardom. They've stayed in their hometown, and are deeply involved in their community, leading something at least resembling a normal life. And – practically right from the start – they've had a support team they can trust: their manager W. Jefferson Holt, and their lawyer, Bertis Downs IV. Together, this team have managed to keep R.E.M. both sane (just about) and solvent.

As Miles Copeland, the head of I.R.S. Records, pointed out in 1994: "The history of the group is no mystery – it was a steady flow upwards. Each album doubled the previous album's sales. And they were not spending fortunes in the studio, and were making money on the road because they didn't have expensive habits. So they were a good, tight little business. They were in the South, they weren't living high. They lived within their means and cut the cloth based on what they were going to generate. Which is how you're supposed to run a business. There are very few artists or managers or lawyers that appreciate that basic fact."

THREE : REALLY EQUAL MEN

The final reason for success: they're friends, and have been for a long time now. Perhaps closer even than family. Which is not to say that they're *friendly* to each other, or that they hang out together all the time; from all accounts, a certain amount of mutual aggression seems to be part of the group dynamic.

But they keep it all together by being utterly democratic, any major decision being made by all of them (including Holt and Downs). This is something which extends even to the songwriting process, according to Robyn Hitchcock: "Their music is done by committee. What's interesting is that the drummer plays guitar and mandolin, and the bassist plays guitar and keyboards – the singer writes the words and the tune but nothing underneath that, so together with Peter, there's three people composing on chord instruments. Their strength is that it's a kind of lattice work. Peter doesn't – in fact, can't – sing. I don't know whether Bill does. The only way they can write a song is by being together. Rather than The Beatles, or Crosby, Stills, Nash & Young – a situation where people are fighting to get *their* track on the album – the songs are very much the four of them. Also, they split the publishing four ways, so they've never had that financial incentive to pull apart from each other."

This is something echoed by former producer Don Dixon: "The democratic aspects of the band are hard to discount as a reason for success. They are an incredibly sensitive bunch. Their ability to fight through serious differences of opinions and problems and stay together for obviously more than financial reasons is laudable. A lot of bands implode under the power of one individual – not everyone can hold their own – but not them."

And, as Bill Berry observed in 1991, after 'Green' had clocked up mega-million sales: "Just by following our own instincts, we've done okay, and that's really what we worry about. It's hard enough pleasing the four of us, to where we're all satisfied that we're finished. What we lack in musicianship we make up for in good taste and sensibility. Basically, we each have an idea of what we *don't* want to do, and that defines our parameters pretty well right there."

FOUR: RADICALS ELUDE MEDIA

Despite unbelievable media focus, they've managed to deal with fame, and the expectations of their audience. This cannot have been easy because, as Michael pointed out in 1991: "It's like, these fine strainers R.E.M. goes through that other performers don't have to go through – these 8,000 word essays on whether or not our integrity is still intact. I'm not complaining, but it seems a little unfair at times, and really a little windy. Who cares, you know? We're a pop band. We write songs: sometimes they're good, sometimes they're not. Sometimes they're great. Years ago we wrote a song that never saw the light of day, and the chorus went: 'It's been a bad day, don't take my picture.' It describes how, if you're a media figure, you can't have bad days and be grumpy and just be left alone every now and then, because suddenly you have an 'attitude', suddenly you have the Garbo thing, suddenly you're eccentric and suddenly every little gesture becomes big, a mystical statement."

The bigger they got, the more that pressure grew. As Peter Buck observed to *Q* in 1992: "Almost all the fans I meet are pretty cool people. They're intelligent and tend to think about things maybe a bit more than your average rock'n'roll fans: sensible people I wouldn't mind having a drink with. But once you're selling like, nine million albums, you're attracting people who aren't really your fans. You start getting the psychos, the people who sit at home and the radio talks to them... "

You also get magazine covers, and the media focused on Stipe in particular. Buck commented in 1995 on the public perception that the group was "Michael's band": "A lot of people think that, and I'm okay with that. I know what I put into the band in terms of songwriting and I know what I take out of it in terms of cheques. It's strange when *Rolling Stone* announce their songwriter of the year: Michael Stipe. Even Michael goes, 'Well, those songs are presented to me to write lyrics to.' It doesn't bother me, but sometimes it can bother, like, my mom. She'll say, 'Peter, *you* should be on the cover of that magazine !' I don't care if I'm never on the cover of a magazine again. And if Michael being on the cover of a magazine can attract attention to a record or a tour or whatever, then I'm fine with that."

But Stipe also gets the downside: his love life gets dissected in public more even than his lyrics or his offhand comments. Is he heterosexual, homosexual, bisexual? "I like sexuality without prefixes," says Stipe, wisely refusing to kiss and tell. His silence won't get them off his back, either. When he didn't do any interviews to promote 'Automatic For The People', it simply fuelled the vicious (and inaccurate) rumour that he had AIDS. Is it any *wonder* this man guards his privacy? Which, of course only adds to the enigma...

FIVE: RAPIDLY ENCROACHING MILLENNIUM

How many more years can they (or will they) keep doing this? Peter Buck once said: "Look, if there comes a time when we're not hip any more, if a trend should arrive that would wipe us off the musical map, I wouldn't have any problems with that. As long as we keep making albums that live up to our own standards and are able to do our thing, even playing in clubs with 200-odd people... that's the way I would like to finish off my career."

Regardless of how many people will be in the audience, group members have said on several occasions that they intend to ring down the final curtain on R.E.M. at midnight of December 31, 1999. Sounds like a good party – I hope I get a ticket.

Meanwhile, what comes next? Tired of the long mixing process involved in 'Monster', Buck has talked wistfully of the possibility of just recording twelve new songs as a live album and putting it out quickly. "It's always been the four of us in a room. So, if we have a bunch of songs with these other guys playing, who knows what it'll sound like?"

With Berry's illness, that live album looks a lot less likely. But whatever the next album proves to be, Buck assured the world in 1994 that R.E.M.'s ideals remain true : "The responsibility is to make whatever we do... to do it as well as we can, and not be condescending to the audience."

So far, so good...

ACKNOWLEDGEMENTS

I've shamelessly plundered all the books listed in the bibliography, plus stacks of *Vox, Q* and *Mojo* magazines. Sometimes I've credited the relevant journalists, sometimes not (due to pressures of time, space, energy, and other cosmic stuff). If I've pissed anybody off, my apologies. All other opinions are mine – and you know what they say about opinions...

Thanks to Chris Charlesworth, for being patient; to Ellie, for being my wife; to Alisa Kwitney (who knows a thing or two about rapid eye movement) for making one dream come true (you only live twice); and to R.E.M., for being R.E.M.

This one goes out to my brother Dave. Just because.

Peter Kenneth* Hogan, July 1995 (* Yes, really.)

R.E.M.

MURMUR

Murmur

RELEASED: APRIL 1983. CURRENT ISSUE: IRS SP 70604

"**D**reams, they complicate/complement my life," Mills and Stipe would sing eight years into their career on Green. And they should know. R.E.M. started life in April 1980 (either without a name at all, or as the Twisted Kites, depending on who you listen to) and had toyed with the idea of various "real offensive" names (Negro Eyes, Slut Bank, Cans Of Piss). "Then we thought we didn't want to be called something that we couldn't tell our parents or have to mumble," Peter Buck later told *Creem* magazine. "R.E.M. just popped out of the dictionary one night. We needed something that wouldn't typecast us because, hell, we didn't know what we were gonna do. So R.E.M. was nice – it didn't lock us in to anything."

Actually, it did. It locked them into something vague and nebulous: dreams, R.E.M. being an acronym for rapid eye movement, the dream phase of sleeping. They even played early gigs as Rapid Eye Movement, although they soon abbreviated the name to R.E.M. And, as much as anything else, it was the obliquely dreamlike imagery of their lyrics that was the key to their appeal.

R.E.M. played every gig and party they could get (Athens was a party town rather than a club town). They acquired a manager, Jefferson Holt, and started playing gigs far and wide – pretty much anywhere that would have

them. It wasn't until a year into their career that they recorded their first single.

After various demos had proved unsatisfactory ("flat and dull," according to Buck), they recorded a single ('Radio Free Europe' b/w 'Sitting Still'), produced by Mitch Easter at his 16-track Drive-In Studios in North Carolina. Easter was recommended by a mutual acquaintance, Peter Holsapple of The dB's, who had been in an earlier band with Easter (and who will reappear in the R.E.M. story much later on). Easter later said that right from the start, "R.E.M. struck me as a real classic singles band." Around the same time Jonny Hibbert, a local lawyer who was planning to start his own record label (Hib-Tone), saw R.E.M. live and offered them a one-off single deal. Hibbert insisted on a different mix of the song from the one Easter had first done (and which the group preferred). "I was probably the last person to override Pete Buck," he says today. Easter also did a 'third' mix and, according to him, the three mixes of the song aren't that different. They would re-record the song for 'Murmur', but the original version was later included on the compilation album 'Eponymous' (and will be discussed further in that chapter).

They gave away many copies of the first pressing (of a thousand copies – it sold six or seven thousand copies in total, through several pressings) for promotional purposes, and this paid off – the record caused enough of a stir among reviewers and college DJs for IRS Records to take notice. The group came to the attention of booking agent Ian Copeland, brother of IRS supremo Miles Copeland, but it was A&R representative Jay Boberg who finally signed them.

To the chagrin of the band's new lawyer, Bertis Downs IV (a friend, newly qualified from law school), R.E.M. had sold Jonny Hibbert all rights (including publishing) to the two songs. R.E.M. bought back the rights as soon as they could (allegedly for $2,000). Hibbert probably later regretted selling, but he had no real choice; Buck swears he would have held good on his threat to bury those songs for ever if Hibbert hadn't sold. Downs also helped them set up their own music publishing company (Night Garden) and their own management company (R.E.M./Athens Ltd.). From now on, Downs was as much a part of the picture as Holt, both treated effectively as band members.

A friend and fan, David Healey, had meanwhile put up the money for three days' recording time at Mitch Easter's Drive-In Studio, hoping to release the results on his own Dasht Hopes label. Five songs were completed: '1,000,000', 'Gardening At Night', 'Carnival Of Sorts (Boxcars)', 'Stumble' and 'Ages Of You' (this last track would be replaced by 'Wolves, Lower' – recorded later – on the finished record). These tracks had already been recorded when the group signed to IRS in May 1982, and their new label promptly released them in August 1982 on a mini-album 'Chronic Town'. These tracks were subsequently made available on 'Dead Letter Office', and will be discussed in that chapter.

Critics liked the single and the mini-album, which sold well enough (20,000 copies in its first year of release) for IRS to give the green light for recording an album. But IRS were nervous about R.E.M. remaining with Easter. They brought in British producer Stephen Hague (best known then for his work with The Human League) and a session took place in Atlanta, which promptly turned into a disaster. One track, 'Catapult', was recorded, but the band hated Hague's approach and the results, for the producer had overdubbed synthesiser parts himself. Fortunately, IRS also disapproved and tentatively agreed to let R.E.M. work with Mitch Easter again, this time in a 24-track studio.

A test track, 'Pilgrimage', was recorded with Mitch Easter and his new engineer/co-producer, Don Dixon at Reflection Studios in Charlotte, North Carolina. Dixon was also immediately impressed with the group: "They were limited musicians technically in some ways, but the vision was very, very acute – the vision was extremely acute, and that's always what I'm looking for."

Perhaps simply to keep the group happy, IRS gave Easter and Dixon the go-ahead. Don Dixon: "I think we understood things about the band the record company didn't. We understood that the combination of their limitations as musicians was a big part of the sound, so you don't just throw those out and go in and put a Curtis Mayfield arrangement on it. It was important for them to understand that we very much liked what they were doing, and we wanted to preserve that over the record company's dead body."

Don Dixon elaborated further in 1994 : "Being both musicians, our approach was to leave as little imprint as possible. We felt like our job was to, as cheaply as possible, reproduce what appeared to be just them playing live. And obviously we knew it couldn't be just them playing live, because that would not be interesting enough. We played little things, little parts here and there. There are certain songs I played on. I think there's some song where both Michael and Bill Berry were playing keyboards – like 'Perfect Circle' – and I'm playing bass on that, and Mitch plays a guitar part here and there. A lot of our job was to get the sound dense and interesting without using fuzz guitars or synthesisers of any kind."

'Murmur' took about 26 days to record, through January and February 1983. Its atmospheric production (some think it murky) earned it the nickname 'Mumble', since many of the lyrics were hard to distinguish. In truth, much of this is down to Michael Stipe's reluctance to sing them any clearer. As a result, some listeners thought he'd improvised the lot and was trying to hide the fact.

Mitch Easter, 1994 : "Michael's lyrics really *were* lyrics – they really were written down. I've even got some of them still on the track sheets. But because everyone liked the band's mysteriousness, they blew it up even more. And I think they thought that we were burning incense in there and it was like speaking in tongues. Maybe there was a bit of vocal improvising, but for the most part he had lyrics – in fact, when we did 'Murmur' he typed them all out on the typewriter at Reflection, because he loved the typewriter there. But I thought his sound was in the grand rock 'n' roll tradition. People would ask me, in all seriousness, what sort of complex electronic technology we were using to, like, muddle his words. We just put a microphone in front of him, and that was the sound he made."

But Stipe's approach was probably a key to the album's (and R.E.M.'s) impact. By leaving things vague, he left the listener to fill in the gaps. Most pop music was (and is) based on the boy/girl relationship; this obviously wasn't. No one was too sure *what* it was based on, but at least it was different, and had a real freshness and vitality. As Peter Buck had said at the time of 'Chronic Town' : "As we went along we realised that we didn't want to be a straight narrative band that has stories in our songs that began and ended. You can put meaning in there – you can write a song about something without ever really referring to what you're writing about – by using evocative phrases, by association of words that you wouldn't normally associate, by repetition, by the power of the music itself and the melodies. You can get the feeling from that experience without ever actually referring to the experience itself."

Don Dixon: "At the time, Michael was particularly self-conscious about the lyrics. He would pull out a matchbook that would have something on it, and that's what he was taking his words from. It wasn't like he was organised. We protected Michael a lot in terms of allowing him to feel completely free in the studio. We gave him his own space that no one could see in. He could turn the lights on and off, he could lay down on the floor and sing if he wanted to. He could do anything he wanted to, and that probably gave him a certain freedom and a kind of confidence that a lot of producers don't understand. Mitch and I understood that, coming from the artist side."

For the group at this point, Easter/Dixon were the ideal producers. And it paid off. Peter Buck: "I remember thinking, 'God, I can't wait until everyone hears this'. It didn't sound like our other records, it didn't sound like us live, and it didn't sound like anything else that was coming out." Emotional, mystical and sublime, it was one heck of a début.

The album cover pictured kudzu, a Japanese vine that grows like wildfire in Georgia, thus proclaiming the band's roots to other Southerners (nit pickers point out that Michael and Peter *aren't* Southerners, actually; so what? The influence is still visible). There were some who felt the lyrics (when distinguishable) also placed them in a Southern context, albeit a literary one, but as Michael told *Melody Maker* in 1984: "I think to compare us to Flannery O'Connor or some of the Southern writers would be maybe pushing it a little too far, but it's kind of nice. We've compared ourselves to Carson McCullers or someone. There's a particular slowness to the South that you don't find in the North or the West Coast or in the Midwest. It's just pretty weird."

'Murmur' made a real impact, largely via college radio. *Rolling Stone* gave it four stars and called it "intelligent, enigmatic, deeply involving ..." They subsequently voted it 'Album Of The Year' and R.E.M. 'Best New Artist'. The album reached number 26 on the US charts – far higher than anyone involved in the project had dared dream.

Michael Stipe, 1994 : "'Murmur' was just a blur for me, I don't remember doing that at all... except for 'Pilgrimage'."

RADIO FREE EUROPE

"Calling all in transit!" A call to arms, a call to party. The song itself is discussed more fully in the entry for 'Eponymous'. This is not the original Hib-tone single, but a re-recorded version that's much more strident and commercial

than the original. Mitch Easter, on the static that begins the track: "We took that static and we keyed it off the bassline so the pulse pattern of the static rhythmically does the same thing that the bass does in the chorus, and we figured that was a good subliminal effect."

PILGRIMAGE

The first track recorded, as a 'test track' (see above); almost a psychedelic rocker.

According to Easter, there are even more of Michael's multi-layered vocals lurking deep in the mix "to make it sound like a Gregorian chant. They're still there, way buried." The song seems to be about the line between superstition and religion. Michael Stipe, in 1985: "'Pilgrimage' still baffles me. At one point right after we recorded it I heard it and it made perfect sense. I was so exhilarated. I thought I had accomplished what I set out to do. And then I forgot!"

LAUGHING

Gently baroque psychedelic folk-rock, with buzzy bass, delicate guitar and perplexing lyrics. Michael has said that the opening line of this song is about Laocoon, a priest of Apollo who tried to stop the Trojans from taking the wooden horse into Troy and who was later – along with both his sons – devoured by sea serpents. ("It was a popular theme in Renaissance painting. There's also John Barth's novel *End Of The Road* where a statue of Laocoon features heavily. Oh, I did change the gender in the song from a man to a woman.") He's also claimed the song is a "rewrite" of Nathaniel Hawthorne's novel *The Scarlet Letter*, and has described it as "violent and brutal" (see his comments on 'The One I Love'). It's been jokingly introduced live as 'Hot As Dick'.

TALK ABOUT THE PASSION

Catchy rock-protest, a song about hunger. The title, plus the line "Not everyone can carry the weight of the world" conjure images of Christ; it's been said that this is also about religious hypocrisy. Features an uncredited female cellist (Easter : "This woman from Charlotte who played in the Symphony down there who somebody at the studio knew"). Peter Buck: "We'd never played it all the way through before. It was just a rehearsal take, and Mitch Easter said, 'That's fine'."

MORAL KIOSK

Choppy riffs, surf licks, booming drums, a weird call and response chorus – this one rocks. Buck has said it too is also about religious hypocrisy. Is the title a pun on moral chaos? Or an Athens in-joke about student notice boards? Why are they banging bits of wood together?

PERFECT CIRCLE

Folky psychedelia, complete with backwards guitar. This also features dual pianos (a grand, played by Mike, and an out-of-tune upright played by Bill), with drums added later. Stipe says it was written about an old girlfriend, while Buck has claimed it had been written about a game of touch football he'd witnessed from the porch of his house one night. He'd been so moved by the spectacle (and frazzled from touring) that he just burst into tears – and later asked Stipe to capture that feeling in song. Whatever, it's still beautiful, though Stipe's explanation makes more sense – it's the closest thing to a straight-out love song on the record. Years later, he called it a "gut-spiller".

CATAPULT

Underrated ode to childhood, with an infectiously dumb chorus. They sound concerned at having been too young to appreciate the Sixties: "Did we miss anything?" Nothing they didn't catch up on later...

SITTING STILL

Another call to action ("Don't waste your time sitting still") with Stipe sounding nasally Dylannish. The B-side to 'Radio Free Europe' (the original Hib-Tone release), remixed and slowed down by Easter, with new backing vocals added. Peter's guitar sounds almost like a harpsichord here.

9-9

A meandering mess, but it has its moments. Stipe: "A song about talking, about conversation and fear of conversation." He's also said it's "not meant to be understood." He gets his wish.

SHAKING THROUGH

Pete Townshend-like introduction, George Harrison-style picking, 'Layla'-style piano, Velvet Underground bass, Roger McGuinn-style vocals – this must be their shopping list! It all adds up to something unique and great, especially when the vocal harmonies blend together towards the end of the second chorus, though only God and Michael Stipe know what it's about.

WE WALK

A really strange one, this. It sounds like a cross between a vaudeville song-and-dance number and a Syd Barrett song, evoking A.A.Milne-like images of childhood. Mitch Easter: "A problematic song. We had a hard time getting it to work. We had to do some

funny stuff to get the basic track to work."
This includes taping Bill Berry playing pool
(recorded in the room below the studio).
Easter: "It was a little song – almost too little.
Somehow the pool balls just made sense."
Allegedly about Michael's friend Dory Duke
(who would walk five steps behind him).

WEST OF THE FIELDS

The fields being the Elysian fields of Greek
myth. They go for a suitably epic approach
to their subject, but it doesn't really come
off. Michael's friend Neill Bogan gets a co-
composer credit as lyricist.

The European 'IRS Years' CD version (IRS
0777 71 3158 2 4) contains four extra tracks:

THERE SHE GOES AGAIN

Cover version of The Velvet Underground
song, recorded straight to two-track. First
released as the B-side to 'Radio Free
Europe' (the IRS version). Not the same as
the version included on 'Dead Letter Office',
where the song is discussed more fully.
Weedy, but charming.

9-9

Energetic live thrash version, produced by Easter
and Dixon. First released as the B-side of the UK
12-inch of '(Don't Go Back To) Rockville'. I like
this a lot better than the studio take.

GARDENING AT NIGHT

Good live version, produced by Easter and
R.E.M. For a discussion of the song, see
'Dead Letter Office'. First released as the
B-side of '(Don't Go Back To) Rockville'
(UK 12-inch).

CATAPULT

So-so live version, produced by "E.D.R. for
The Source". First released as the B-side of
the US 7-inch of '(Don't Go Back To)
Rockville'.

RECKONING/FILE
UNDER WATER

RELEASED APRIL 1984. CURRENT ISSUE: IRS CDA 7045.

Following the release of 'Murmur', the group continued to tour incessantly, playing their first stadium dates as support to The Police ("the most wretched, miserable experience of our lives") and briefly making their first forays into Britain (*NME* called them "the most vital American group of today") and France.

In December 1983 they returned to Reflection Sound Studios in Charlotte to record 'Murmur's sequel, again with Easter and Dixon co-producing. The results are much more immediately accessible and listenable than the first album, downright poppy at times – perhaps the fact that it was recorded over the Christmas period means that it carries a bit of implicit seasonal jollity with it (possibly as a result of seasonal indulgence). Recording took between eleven and twenty-five days (since some of these were eighteen-hour days, maybe they all just lost count).

What made the biggest difference this time was their confidence in their material (they'd been writing like demons), all of which had been thoroughly road-tested live. Bill

Berry: "As far as I was concerned, I knew when we walked in on the first day that the songs were better than the ones on the first album, so I wasn't worried."

Mitch Easter: "They were playing more and more. 'Reckoning' does have a bit more of a direct sound. I don't think it was really a master plan, y'know, I just think it was a case of the songs they had at the time being more straight-ahead. In the studio, we just tried to treat them appropriately." Certainly, there's greater production clarity this time, and the songs are more obviously commercial and immediate.

Even so, according to Don Dixon, Michael Stipe was undergoing "a bit of an identity crisis". Michael himself later described the sessions as "a 12-day drunken party. No sleep, just staying up and staying drunk or whatever." (On the other hand, Easter recalls the sessions as "pretty sedate").

Dixon recounts that Michael was "worried about his health after the long bouts of touring, and a friend had gotten him on this garlic thing. He was eating cloves of garlic like apples. We had to de-garlic the microphone after. That mike had its own little room for a while. We had to air it out."

Peter Buck told *Jamming!* magazine : "With 'Reckoning' there's a whole lot of weirdness about lost love or lost friends, because we've had a couple of suicides and car wrecks and stuff like that which happened to close friends. And communication – there are a number of songs about communication."

Michael Stipe, 1994: "That whole record was about movement and travelling, perpetual motion. I read a review that said this, and suddenly it all made sense to me. I didn't realise as they were going down on tape that every song had that thing in common. From that moment on I was acutely aware of what I was writing and all the records became very thematic and it's all very much on purpose."

Some of the songs here pre-date 'Murmur', but hadn't fitted with that album's distinctive atmosphere.

The album cover painting was by Georgia folk artist the Reverend Howard Finster, in collaboration with Michael Stipe. The album's title? Buck phrased it succinctly: "The second album shows the world whether you're dealing with a worthless bunch of talentless hacks who had a lucky idea, or a good band. It was our day of reckoning. This had to be something that would find you or leave you cold." On the spine were the words of the album's alternate title: *File under water* ("water is passage, journey, change," said Buck).

The press loved it, the most notable review coming from the *NME*'s Mat Snow: "When I get to heaven, the angels will be playing not harps but Rickenbackers. And they will be playing songs by R.E.M." Peter Buck almost certainly got to the point where he was sick of seeing the word 'Rickenbacker' in print; Byrds comparisons were similarly rife.

'Reckoning' reached number 27 on the US charts, and remained in the Top 200 for over a year.

HARBORCOAT

A swinging rocker, with an epic feel. In 1984, Peter Buck said the title referred to "A type of protection. It's rather like being invisible, maybe in an emotional way." Michael Stipe added, "It's not necessarily a protection against wind or cold. It could be less tangible things." Yet Stipe is bidding the 'harborcoat' farewell, telling himself to "react". Possibly this is a song of mourning, or of alienation. Buck finally admitted in 1988 that he "never understood what 'Harborcoat' was about." Stipe has since referred to the song as being "violent and brutal" (see entry for 'The One I Love' on 'Document').

7 CHINESE BROTHERS

This one had already been written at the time of 'Murmur'. It was inspired by a children's fable by Claire Huchet Bishop and Kurt Wiese titled *The Five Chinese Brothers*, and it does indeed sound vaguely Chinese. More water imagery here (one brother could hold the ocean in his mouth). "She will return," could refer to a broken relationship, or to reincarnation. It somehow reminds me of The Soft Machine's 'Joy Of A Toy'.

SO. CENTRAL RAIN

And yet more water, this time referring to spring flooding in Athens. But it's also a flood of tears, a farewell – as is 'Camera' – to Michael's friend Carol Levy, a photographer who had taken the back cover photo for the Hib-Tone single and who had died in a car accident. Lines like "Did you never call? I waited for your call" and "I'm so sorry" convey the regret of things left unsaid and unresolved. The accidental vocal fade may well have been caused by sheer grief – after emitting the last of a series of strangled moans, Michael Stipe fell down the stairs on which he was singing, breaking the microphone in the process. Originally titled 'Southern Central Rain'.

PRETTY PERSUASION

Straightforward rocker, supposedly inspired by a recurring dream of Michael's, in which he photographed The Rolling Stones sitting on a dock for a record sleeve. Not that you can tell that from the words...

TIME AFTER TIME (ANNELISE)

Slow and graceful, this countryish ballad sounds like The Byrds swapping guitar mantras with The Velvet Underground. The "water tower" referred to may be the same one (in Athens) where Mike Mills was arrested for "cavorting nude with a young lady" several years later.

SECOND GUESSING

Energetic rocker that's a bitter jibe at those who are wise (or fashionable) with hindsight. It would seem to be attacking hype and hypocrisy, bandwagon-jumpers, and unwanted media attention.

LETTER NEVER SENT

The ceaseless touring gave them chronic homesickness – hence the daydreams of a "vacation in Athens", and this fast-paced (but unsent) love letter home.

CAMERA

Another farewell to the late Carol Levy ("will she be remembered?"), this one slow and mournful.

(DON'T GO BACK TO) ROCKVILLE

Robyn Hitchcock: "The only song any one of them claims to have written by themselves." Written by Mike Mills, in fact, for the benefit of a girl named Ingrid Schorr from Rockville, Maryland, who was planning to leave Athens to return home in the summer of 1980. Written then, and so one of the few early R.E.M. songs to be released, though in much altered form – it was originally much faster (Easter: "semi-punk"). The group had tired of it until the country music-loving Bertis Downs suggested they slow it down from its stage thrash incarnation into a countryish Byrdsian lament. They claim they did it as a joke. Doesn't matter – it's still a great pop song, from the honky-tonk piano to the exquisite lyrics, which veer from the overconfident ("I believe you'll be coming back before too long") to the self-defeating ("it's not as

though I really need you"). I had a globetrotting girlfriend in 1984, and this song scarcely ever left the turntable.

LITTLE AMERICA

Manic strut, a pile-up of images of life on the road. Just when you think it can't get any faster, it does, Buck punctuating the air like a siren. R.E.M. had seen a lot of America in the previous couple of years. "Jefferson, I think we're lost," is generally assumed to refer to the band's manager Jefferson Holt, but it makes as much (or more) sense applied to President Thomas Jefferson, a man who wanted his country to be so much more than it is.

The European 'IRS Years' CD version (IRS 0777 7 13159 2 3) contains five extra tracks:

WIND OUT

"With friends" says the subtitle, these being Jefferson Holt and Bertis Downs on vocals. A surf thrash with almost no redeeming features. Recorded live to two-track. 'Reckoning' outtake; see 'Dead Letter Office' for alternate version.

PRETTY PERSUASION

Messy early version. Recorded live to track, 17/2/83.

WHITE TORNADO

Dynamic speed drumming introduces messy surf instrumental, recorded live to two-track. See 'Dead Letter Office' for alternate version.

TIGHTEN UP

'Murmur' outtake, recorded live to track, 17/2/83. Cover version of a song by Northern Soul heroes Archie Bell and The Drells. R.E.M.'s version features weedy (minimal) vocals, Mitch Easter on xylophone, and was first released on a flexidisc given free with the magazine *Bucketful Of Brains*.

MOON RIVER

Another 'Murmur' outtake, recorded live to track, 17/2/83. Written by Henry Mancini and Johnny Mercer, this became Andy Williams' theme tune but was first sung by Audrey Hepburn in the film version of Truman Capote's *Breakfast At Tiffany's*. A staple of the band's live set for years, their version sounds so much like a demo, the vocals so tentative, that you'd think Stipe was writing the song as he sings. It fades with a weird organ flourish that seems totally out of place. Idiosyncratic, but charming. Michael: "Even as a little boy, it made me kind of want to cry or be by myself for a while. I think it's a really special song that can do that." Stipe apparently used to think that "huckleberry friend" referred to Huckleberry Hound. That makes two of us ...

FABLES OF THE RECONSTRUCTION/ RECONSTRUCTION OF THE FABLES

RELEASED JUNE 1985. CURRENT ISSUE: IRS DMIRF 1003

The traditionally 'difficult' third album, for which R.E.M. would finally abandon their partnership with Mitch Easter and Don Dixon – a choice made partly because Easter was on the road with his band, Let's Active. And perhaps because they simply felt it was time for a change. Mitch Easter: "No one ever believes me when I say this, but R.E.M. going on to use other producers was just fine with me. It was the thing to do. Either way it would have been fine with me. All I really wanted to do was the follow-up to the single, and I did that. By the time we had done the two albums, it made sense for them to move on." Don Dixon : "There was only so far we could go, and they needed to be moving in a forward direction. I'm not sure we could have done that for them."

Suggestions for a possible replacement producer included Elvis Costello and Van Dyke Parks (either of whom would have been interesting), but in the end it was decided that they would use Joe Boyd. Boyd was Peter Buck's choice – simply because he'd produced a good many folk-influenced albums that Buck loved (by Nick Drake and Fairport Convention, to name but two). Easter later commented: "I thought it was a real hip choice, and I thought it made sense."

Initially, it appeared that Boyd was also otherwise engaged, producing Mary Margaret O'Hara. When she cancelled her sessions, Boyd flew to Athens, and recorded some trial 8-track demos with R.E.M. "They liked my approach," he later recalled. "I don't try to put hands on the music. I try to create the right atmosphere for the artist to do what they want. I'm not going to spend three days getting a drum sound."

The songs at this point were only partly written. When finished, they would conjure an atmosphere of Southern Gothic, of elegant decay. Many were character-based stories, and Buck later described it as "Michael's storytelling record". Michael Stipe, in 1985: "I found myself surrounded a whole lot when we were writing these songs by fables and nursery rhymes and Uncle Remus and old tales. The idea of stories being passed down and becoming a tradition and having those stories become as much a part of a way of living or a particular area that you live in as the religion or the trees or the weather – I like the connection between that and the South."

Boyd was based in London, and so the group flew in that March, which was rainy and cold. They rented a flat in Mayfair, and commuted to Livingstone Studios in Wood Green, North London. The experience was not a happy one. 'Reckoning' had begun confidently (due to a stack of good material that they knew backwards). This time they were road weary beyond belief and had practically no

PAGE 20

material. Boyd also felt insecure and unsure that he could improve on the sound of the first two albums, and he also seemed caught between the band's wishes and those of IRS.

They discarded at least nine songs they'd brought in as being below par, and created seven new ones from scratch in the studio. Peter Buck later revealed that, "It's the only time we've walked in and didn't have a clue. We had this batch of songs that we'd written really fast, with not even the beginning of an idea on how to make them. We couldn't agree on tempos, we'd argue about things like keys... We forgot some of the things you have to remember like you have to know what you're doing."

They were unused to working this way, with material as yet untried in a live setting. And the pressure took its toll. Stipe would later claim he'd suffered a "mental, nervous, physical and mechanical breakdown" during this period. And the others weren't in good shape either. In 1987, Buck told *Bucketful Of Brains*: "I had a miserable time making that album. We were all miserable and mean to each other. If there ever was a point in our career where we thought we were sick to

that, but we were a mile from the Tube station so I had to carry my guitar in the snow to the Tube. I had to stand up the whole way, then walk a mile to the studio. I wasn't sleeping, I slept about an hour a night and I drank all the time. If I didn't feel bad anyway, that was enough to make me feel crummy. That record just reflects that perfectly, it's a misery album in a lot of ways – but I like it, the songwriting's great. It's one of our stronger albums as far as songwriting." Stipe called the record "dark, dank and paranoid", a reflection of his mood at the time.

Despite the problems, Joe Boyd remembers the sessions fondly; in 1994 he reminisced to *Mojo* magazine: "Michael was a bit wary at first, but when he discovered I'd met Brion Gyson and that I knew what cut-ups were, everything was okay. That made sense of his approach to lyrics which, in those days much more than now, were very like a string of phrases that have been cut up and shuffled and put back together. He didn't want the lyrics too closely examined and wouldn't have the words on the sleeve. There was a lot of 'pull the voice back!' when we were mixing. Same with the guitar. With a lot of groups,

death of each other, that was it. We had just got off an eight-and-a-half month tour, we rehearsed for eight or nine days and wrote these fifteen songs, being home for a week and a half – the first time in a year. We flew over to London and it rained all the time, it's winter, it's snowing. We didn't have enough money to rent cars and shit, so we had to take the Tube – and there's nothing wrong with everyone wants their bit louder. With R.E.M. everyone wanted it quieter. It made it very difficult for me to get a vivid image in my mind, and ideal mix, as I kept getting knocked sideways by 'Don't turn up the voice! Don't turn up the guitar!' What they were after was the blend. They saw themselves as an ensemble from which no one part stuck out. They're incredibly smart and it works."

The album also featured three string players, and three brass players (including Pete Thomas, who'd later work with Joe Jackson and Richard Thompson).

Although reviews were good (most finding it a more mature work than its predecessors), the group themselves remained dubious as to its merits. Joe Boyd, 1994: "I always felt frustrated that I didn't get a better record. There was a raw energy about the first two albums that this one lacked a little bit. I would have liked it to have a better sound. When it first came out it got good reviews and sold very well. Then about a year later the group started talking about it as a disappointment in their interviews. I didn't really blame them. But now the revisionist view is that it is quite a good record, and a lot of people come

up to me and say, 'I wasn't sure at first, but now I think it's one of their best records.' Even Michael has said that to me. He now thinks it's a great record. So that pleases me."

As to their aspirations for their music at the time, Buck told the *NME* : "I'm more famous now than I'd ever like to be. What I'm really looking for, ideally, is that ten years down the line people will think we did something really incredible. Even if it's overlooked now, we will have done something that's so strong it will cross all boundaries. So that in ten years people will listen to it like I listen to The Velvet Underground or The Doors or Muddy Waters." Ten years on, 'Fables Of The Reconstruction' still stands up well.

The circular title? Though 'reconstruction' has connotations of the post-Civil War South, it was also at the time a Reagan-administration buzzword: one which turned out to be a fable. Working titles for the album were 'The Sound And The Fury' (taken from *King Lear* and previously used as the title to a novel by William Faulkner), and 'High On Drugs' (one suspects this one was a wind-up, simply to annoy IRS). 'Fables' outsold 'Reckoning' and picked up the New Music Award for 'Album Of The Year'.

FEELING GRAVITYS PULL

Michael Stipe, 1986: "'Feeling Gravitys Pull' came from a hand gesture. I just saw it, and then I wrote a song around it. I really focus on detail more than the grand picture, and that detail is what becomes the words of the song." Another "gut-spiller" according to Stipe, which conjures up echoes of alienation, from the television-style guitar to the brooding cello to the drums like thunderclouds; fortunately, the bridge soars along with the strings, giving at least some feeling of hope. "It's a Man-Ray kind of sky" refers to a work by the surrealist photographer/artist titled *Observatory Time: The Lovers*. The lack of an apostrophe in the song's title is presumably intentional (as with 'Lifes Rich Pageant', it's hard to tell with R.E.M.).

MAPS AND LEGENDS

Baroque folk-rock, that sounds like an attempt at compassion ("maybe these maps and legends may be misunderstood"). Michael Stipe, 1985: "There are a lot of people (who are) like maps. You look at them, and you can lay them out on a table and read them and run your finger over them. You can find their little stories, their little squares and circles. Some are filled in, some are not. Some have lines connecting them, and it's real pretty, nice and mysterious, but you can't make head or tail of it. So, then, when you've done with that, you go down to the key and it tells you what the circle means. And then you look at the map and it starts to make sense. There are lot of people like that." Stipe has also said the song is "kind of about" the Reverend Howard Finster (the cover artist of 'Reckoning').

DRIVER 8

A great folk/country train song: "Southern Crescent" is a railway line that runs through Georgia. Peter Buck: "We all live near the train tracks, so we hear trains all the time." They've compared it in live introductions to Jimmy Webb's 'Wichita Lineman' i.e. a romantic look at the working life ("we've been on this shift too long"). Michael has also compared the "destination" referred to in the song as "something that's almost unobtainable, it's almost an idea, almost this fantasy or this dream, and you're fooling yourself into believing that it's almost obtainable, when in fact it really isn't."

LIFE AND HOW TO LIVE IT

The first vaguely rocky track. Inspired by a magazine article Michael had read, about a schizophrenic man whose apartment was divided into two halves, each furnished with two sets of everything, each half thus reflecting a different aspect of his personality. When he died, copies of his self-published book *Life How To Live* were found on the premises.

OLD MAN KENSEY

Another true-life story: Kensey was an assistant to the Reverend Howard Finster and a bit of a 'character', well known for his eccentric pranks. Peter Buck: "He had to be fired, because he was a dog kidnapper. He would ransom the dogs, get all the money and go out and get drunk. That was one of the more clever ideas that he had." Jerry Ayers of Limbo District (another Athens group) gets a co-composer credit for this one. Old Man Kensey can be seen (just) in the background of the photograph of Finster on the sleeve of 'Reckoning'. Even more so than with the opening track, a feeling of paranoia and depression seeps through.

CAN'T GET THERE FROM HERE

A "jazz ballad", according to Peter Buck, who also said, "It's like a tongue-in-cheek tribute to Ray Charles and James Brown and all the other great Georgia music giants." "It's about where to go to unwind," said Mike Mills. Thankfully, this one is upbeat and rocky, with horns and a soulful growl from Stipe. Michael told *Tasty World* : "I was thinking of sounding like Mahalia Jackson. I tried to do as many different voices on the album as possible. On ('Can't Get There From Here') I can pick five different voices. I had to show them how to do that (the jazz horn squeal at the end). I said, 'I want you to sound like Louis Armstrong'. They didn't understand. I had to use my mouth and go 'Waaah Waaaah-Waah', and they thought I meant his trumpet sound. What I really meant was his voice! They were really confused."

The title is an old Irish joke (one of Shirley Maclaine's loopier books bears the title *You Can Get There From Here,* thus denoting a lack of humour on her part).

GREEN GROW THE RUSHES

Folky protest, with gorgeous guitar fills reminiscent of '7 Chinese Brothers'. Working title (pre-lyrics) was 'The Happy Carpenter Song'. Takes its finished title from the Scottish folk song (words by Robert Burns). Stipe stated that this was sung by American troops in Mexico during the Mexican war of 1846, which earned them the nickname 'gringo'. No,

I don't believe it either. Nor does Marcus Gray, who points out that the song sung in Mexico was actually 'Green Grow The Laurels' (another folk song), and that 'gringo' is simply the Spanish word for 'foreigner'. Anyway, Stipe has said that *this* song is about the plight of Mexican workers in the USA.

KOHOUTEK

Kohoutek is a comet, discovered by the Czech astronomer Dr Lubos Kohoutek in 1973. When it approached Earth in January 1974, many feared the end of the world; instead, the very unspectacular-looking ice-bomb missed us by a spectacular distance. It won't return for another ten million years. This almost discordant folk ballad about a presumably failed romance is probably named after the comet simply to convey a sense of anticlimax.

AUCTIONEER (ANOTHER ENGINE)

Fairly tuneless rocker that combines train imagery with that of the auction (possibly to convey images of the slave trade). Michael

Stipe, 1985: "I wrote it on a train when I couldn't sleep. I returned to it three months later and I had no idea where it came from. I only put it together on that train trip at three in the morning after leaving my girlfriend." Whose name was Caroline, and who remained a friend – she appears in the videos for 'The One I Love' and 'Pop Song '89'.

GOOD ADVICES

Poignant ballad about homesickness and infidelity on the road.

WENDELL GEE

According to Peter Buck, between Athens and Gainsville (where R.E.M. filmed the *Left Of Reckoning* video), "There's a whole town, everyone's last name in it is Gee, apparently. There's Wendell Gee Used Cars, and there's Gwen Gee's Pool Hall, and there's Roy Gee Bail Bondsman ..." Graceful, haunting ballad in the same vein as The Byrds' 'Old John Robertson'. In 1995 Stipe described this as being one of his "vomit songs": "Sometimes I just open my mouth and *blaagh*, there it is on the page. Like a bullet train." I'd say this is not only the best track on the album, but one of their finest ever songs. Peter Buck reportedly hates it.

The European 'IRS Years' CD version (IRS 0777 7 13160 2 9) contains five extra tracks, all B-sides :

CRAZY

Outtake from 'Fables', a cover version of a Pylon song. Unable to remember all the words, Michael improvised his own. Remixed by Steve Fjelstad. First released as the B-side of 'Wendell Gee' (UK 12-inch); also included on 'Dead Letter Office'.

BURNING HELL

Another 'Fables' outtake, first released as the B-side of 'Can't Get There From Here' (UK 12-inch); also included on 'Dead Letter Office', and discussed more fully there.

BANDWAGON

Another 'Fables' outtake, first released as the B-side of 'Can't Get There From Here' (UK 12-inch); also included on 'Dead Letter Office', and discussed more fully there.

DRIVER 8

Patchy live version, recorded in Seattle, 27/6/84. Produced by "E.D.R. for The Source". First released as the B-side of 'Wendell Gee' (UK 12-inch).

MAPS AND LEGENDS

Good acoustic live version, recorded on cassette 24/5/87 at Texas Records, which proves the song is strong enough to stand without the string arrangement. First released as the B-side to 'The One I Love'.

LIFES RICH PAGEANT
R.E.M.

LIFES RICH PAGEANT

RELEASED JULY 1986. CURRENT ISSUE: IRS DMIRG 7014

Peter Buck, 1992: "There was a time in 1985 when we'd been on the road for five-and-a-half years, and it was kind of tense. Everyone was tired of being away from home, and broke, and always in each other's company. We were staying at cheapo motels, and sometimes you'd get a quart of beer and sit on your own in the parking lot. That would be the only time you could be alone for a week. It reached a point where we were totally ambivalent about going on."

In an attempt to fire themselves up from this low point, R.E.M. decided to try working with another new producer, Don Gehman, in the hope of coming up with a more commercial formula (he'd worked with The Bee Gees, and had most recently produced John Cougar Mellencamp).

During 1994, Gehman recalled to *Mojo*: "I felt that R.E.M. were great songwriters and had a great mystique, but a lot of the power was lost – they weren't able to get things across in a real direct manner. That was the essence of the whole experience for both of us, I think, this conflict of my idea of how to make something direct, and their idea about the fact that things weren't really supposed to be that way. So the result is what happened.

"I think 'Lifes Rich Pageant' was the first thing that had actually been recorded at John Mellencamp's studio other than John's record, 'Scarecrow'. Their material was prepared except for the lyrics. And it wasn't really presented to me, which was unusual for me as well. They had worked out – the three of them, aside from Michael – all the music, and I think Michael had heard everything but only wrote the lyrics in the studio."

In fact, once again they didn't have enough new songs (proof that touring destroys the creative spirit), and were forced to revitalise some old ones. Recording took place over a three-week period in April 1986, at Mellencamp's studio in Bloomington, Indiana (the album would subsequently be mixed in L.A.). During recording, both Gehman and the band were staying at a golf course, with apartments on a lake. To further help them restore lost energy, Gehman restricted studio hours to an eight-hour working day.

Gehman felt his priorities were clear: "I wasn't real interested in the music being perfect – I was more interested in providing a little bit more clarity to Michael's voice, that was what I was really shooting for. And they were probably ready for it. It was my duty to prove the point that it could be done in a way that didn't lose any of the mystery and the mystique that they thought was so important to the band."

This meant pinning Michael down, and making him rethink his whole attitude to singing. Stipe later said that, "Don was the first person that hauled me aside and questioned what I was doing. That can be really good, to have some objective voice saying, 'Why are you choosing to say this? Why are you singing what you are?' A lot of the time it was rhetorical, it wasn't the kind of thing I had to answer to, but he would just place the seed for me to think about change."

The result was noticeably more upfront vocals. There was another change in the vocals as well: lyrically (though still obscure) they seemed a lot more politically conscious.

Though the partnership with Gehman seemed like a meeting of opposites, for both parties it proved fruitful. In 1994 Gehman stated: "They were totally different than anyone I'd ever worked with. It was kind of like a spiritual experience for me, looking back on it. Because they didn't have any of the rock'n' roll baggage that I was used to dealing with – wanting to make a hit record, caring about ego things, the rock star image – all of those things were just not present here. These people were kind of living in the moment – which I consider a very high state, spiritually. They were willing to just go along with the process. And whatever came out of it, if they liked it they kept it, if they didn't, they tried something else. It taught me to get out of the plan and open up my eyes and ears."

Peter Buck was more guarded: "I think we made the perfect record that we could in that style." He was also later scathing about the lack of support the band had received from MCA Records (which was then still distributing IRS): "I remember being told by MCA's Head of Promotions that 'We're not going to promote this record because there aren't any hit singles'."

Irritatingly, the songs have a different running order than those indicated on the sleeve;

this is partly because two extra songs were included at the last minute, and partly through wilful obscurity (the CD sleeve has not been amended).

The album's title was a phrase uttered by Peter Sellers' Inspector Clouseau in *A Shot In The Dark*. Its lack of an apostrophe was apparently accidental (though it's often hard to tell with R.E.M.). The album cover combined half a photograph of Bill Berry with a drawing of a bison (i.e. Buffalo Bill).

Reviews were mixed, but sales were good: the album reached 21 on the US charts, and shifted over half a million copies.

BEGIN THE BEGIN

Driving rocker, with the clarity of Michael's vocals coming as quite a shock after the earlier work. Peter Buck, 1986: "Written with all of us on acoustic guitars in Michael's living room. We had twenty degrees weather, and we were all huddled up in our jackets, trying to write songs for the album. I had that one little riff and that was it. We just kind of sat and made it up, and we went, 'Let's change this, let's make it so it never repeats'. The original version was about a minute longer and *nothing* was the same all the way through except the riff. There were five different choruses, no bridge, no melody." The title is a pun on Cole Porter's 'Begin The Beguine', and indicates a call for action. Rich in American mythology (Miles Standish was one of the leaders of the Pilgrim Fathers); "the insurgency began and we missed it" seems to refer to the Sixties and/or the American revolution. You kind of feel they're calling for another one (of each?).

ancient Gauls used to fear the sky would fall on their heads (see any *Asterix* book); Chicken Licken feared that it already had. There seem to be references to Galileo's experiments with gravity, but both Stipe and Berry have said this one's about acid rain. It could also be taken as being about a simple awe of nature, the kind we city folk forget (and look where that's got us). Defusing all the profundity, the wonderfully funny backing vocals ask, "What is it up in the air for?" Amazingly, this epic rocker failed to make much impact as a single.

THESE DAYS

This keeps up the manic pace, and seems to be a general purpose protest song. "We are hope despite the times," Stipe sings, talkin' 'bout his generation. Live, he's introduced it as a "moralistic tale", also comparing it to Aesop's 'Fables'. Fishy imagery, but why is anybody's guess.

CUYAHOGA

Gentle ballad that calls for the repair of America, both politically and ecologically. The title is the Native American name for a river in Ohio so polluted that it sometimes catches fire. Michael: "We destroyed a culture to build ours."

FALL ON ME

"This may well be my favourite song in the R.E.M. catalogue," Michael Stipe announces during the band's 1991 *Unplugged* show. The

HYENA

A canine fable that (appropriately) dates back to 'Fables Of The Reconstruction'. An anti-nuke song ("The only thing we fear is fearlessness," is a paraphrase of Franklin D. Roosevelt). Fairly average rocker.

UNDERNEATH THE BUNKER

Instrumental (mainly) written during the 'Fables' sessions. According to Peter Buck, things were going badly in the studio, so the band took a break: "We went to this Greek restaurant and got drunk, and this is the type of stuff they were playing. We just came back and did our own version of that kind of music." Actually, it sounds Turkish.

THE FLOWERS OF GUATEMALA

Despite the floral imagery, this would seem to be about US intervention in Central America. In concert Michael declared that both 'Green Grow The Rushes' and 'Hyena' were also about this subject: "There's big fish and medium fish and little fish. Big Fish is the United States; Medium Fish is Mexico; Little Fish is Guatemala. One eats the other one up. One gets bigger ... " Sounds like one of the gentler Velvet Underground songs.

I BELIEVE

Banjo interlude introduces a bouncily poppy catalogue of affirmation. This is a rewritten version of an earlier song, 'When I Was Young', which was dropped from 'Fables' at the last minute (but too late to remove the title from early printings of the album sleeve). The lyrics seem like teasing glimpses of autobiography ("I will not tell!"), and encouragement/advice to those who follow after. The title came from a Mahalia Jackson gospel song of the same name, a snippet of which Michael would sing a cappella as an introduction when performing this live.

WHAT IF WE GIVE IT AWAY

Bluesy swinger. This one dates back to 1981, and was previously titled 'Get On Their Way'. "Here's the trailer's home" refers to the fact that Michael Stipe lived in a trailer park just prior to joining R.E.M.

JUST A TOUCH

A really old song – it dates back to 1980. Supposedly based on a true incident witnessed by Stipe when he was 17 and working

SWAN SWAN H

Written on the tour bus in November 1985 at three in the morning, and described by Peter Buck as "fake Irish music. We had this stuff, and I just started playing it and Michael said, 'Yeah, I've got words that will fit that!' We worked it out in about twenty minutes." The words were taken from a 1920s book that Michael had found, about post-Civil War hymns of the emancipated slaves. The result is a sweeping folk ballad that seems part gibberish, part Civil War imagery. The title was, according to Stipe, supposed to be pronounced 'Swan Swan Huh' (rather than aitch). Mike Mills (correctly) thought this "too far towards pretension."

as a busboy in a disco-restaurant called Sonny And Cher's. On the day Elvis Presley died, an Elvis impersonator named Orion was playing at the restaurant and was showered with flowers at the end of his set by grieving female Presley fans. "I'm so goddamn young" is a quote from Patti Smith's 'Privileges (Set Me Free)', which fits well with the general punk vibe (three chords and an attitude), as does the cheesy organ break.

SUPERMAN

Uncredited on the album sleeve, this cover version of a B-side by Sixties Texas garage band The Clique (written by G. Zekley and M. Bottler) features Mike Mills' début as lead vocalist. Buck had unearthed the original single while working in a record store years before ("I gave Mike a copy, and we've both loved that song for six years, ever since 1980.

This song has two chords, and it took us that long to work it out"). It's a wonderful slice of pop at its dumbest and most compulsive, a mock-macho obsession song (sounds like things are not going that well between Lois & Clark) that's easily the best thing on the album, and which understandably made quite an impact when it was released as a single.

The European 'IRS Years' CD (IRS 0777 7 13201 2 5) contains six additional tracks:

TIRED OF SINGING TROUBLE

Short but enjoyable blues stomper that's almost a cappella (minimum accompaniment). Previously unreleased, an outtake from 'Lifes Rich Pageant'.

ROTARY TEN

Outtake from 'Lifes Rich Pageant'. First released as the B-side to 'Fall On Me' (US 7-inch), also included on 'Dead Letter Office', and discussed more fully there.

TOYS IN THE ATTIC

Cover of an Aerosmith song. First released as the B-side to 'Fall On Me' (UK 12-inch), also included on 'Dead Letter Office', and discussed more fully there.

JUST A TOUCH

Rudimentary live in the studio version, recorded straight to two-track during the 'Reckoning' sessions. Previously unreleased (for a pretty good reason!)

DREAM (ALL I HAVE TO DO)

Haphazard acoustic version of the Boudleaux Bryant song made famous by The Everly Brothers. Taken from the soundtrack of the movie Athens Ga. Inside/Out , produced by Bill Cody. Michael has said that he hates this song. It shows.

SWAN SWAN H

Good acoustic version, taken from the soundtrack of Athens Ga. Inside/Out , produced by Bill Cody.

DEAD LETTER OFFICE

R.E.M.

DEAD LETTER OFFICE

RELEASED APRIL 1987. CURRENT ISSUE: IRS CDA 70054

Subtitled "a virtuous compost, Being a Compendium Of Oddities Collared, and B-sides compiled" – and that pretty much sums it up. It's possible that IRS were keen on this project happening simply in order to stem the tide of R.E.M. bootlegs. Regardless, it's an enjoyable mixture and was at least intelligently compiled (by Peter Buck, who also provided self-deprecatingly witty sleeve notes). "Listening to this album should be like browsing through a junk shop," he wrote – and so it is: some rubbish, some buried treasure. Though recording quality varies a lot (some of this was never produced as such, merely recorded straight to two-track), the delights by far outweigh the dross .

CRAZY

Melancholy pop: a cover version of an old Pylon number, and an outtake from 'Fables', produced by Joe Boyd. Unable to contact Pylon to learn the words, Michael improvised. First released as the B-side of 'Driver 8' in the US, and of 'Wendell Gee' in the UK.

THERE SHE GOES AGAIN

Fairly faithful cover of The Velvet Underground song, and a 'Murmur' outtake. This sounds slightly more echoing than the version released as the B-side to 'Radio Free Europe' (the IRS version) – possibly a mix or even an alternate take? Recorded straight to two-track. Second acoustic guitar by Mitch Easter.

BURNING DOWN

A 'Reckoning' outtake, remixed by Steve Fjelstad. First released as the B-side of the UK double pack single of 'Wendell Gee'. With images like "plantations burning", the song evokes the Civil War era. A medium-paced rocker.

VOICE OF HAROLD

An alternate version of '7 Chinese Brothers', recorded in the same session as a warm-up and featuring the same backing track with Michael singing 'lyrics' taken from the back cover sleeve notes of a gospel record that was lying around in the studio: The Revelaires' *The Joy Of Knowing Jesus*. I actually prefer this to the finished version. First released as the B-side of 'So. Central Rain' (UK 12-inch).

BURNING HELL

Another 'Fables' outtake: a heavy metal pastiche, written solely so that Peter could use his new fuzzbox. First released as the B-side of 'Can't Get There From Here' (UK 12-inch).

WHITE TORNADO

First released as the B-side of 'Superman': a minor-league surf instrumental recorded in the same session as the Hib-Tone single, and one of the few early R.E.M. songs to be recorded. Working/alternate titles for this were 'Stronger Than Dirt' and 'Generic Surf Song'.

TOYS IN THE ATTIC

An Aerosmith cover! "Always fun to play live," writes Peter. Fun to listen to, too – R.E.M. deflate the pomposity (almost). Outtake from 'Lifes Rich Pageant', produced by Don Gehman. First released as the B-side of 'Fall On Me' (UK 12-inch).

WINDOUT

'Reckoning' outtake, but the song dates back to 1980. A surf/punk thrash that ended up on the soundtrack to *Bachelor Party*.

AGES OF YOU

A 'Reckoning' outtake, remixed by Steve Fjelstad. This is a rewrite of 'Burning Down', but is a lot more fun. First released as the B-side of the UK double pack single of 'Wendell Gee'.

PALE BLUE EYES

"One of my favourite Lou Reed songs," writes Peter. Drastically altered lyrics by Michael, which annoys Velvets purists (a good enough reason for him to do it).

Raggedly wonderful. A 'Reckoning' outtake, recorded live to two-track.

ROTARY TEN

Written during the 'Fables' sessions, and an outtake from 'Lifes Rich Pageant'. "A Henry Mancini spy movie theme," said Michael Stipe (blame a diet of too many *Pink Panther* movies while they were recording the album), though actually it sounds more like the theme for something starring Edgar Lustgarten. First released as the B-side of 'Fall On Me'. Not to be confused with 'Rotary Eleven' (the B-side of 'Losing My Religion').

BANDWAGON

An outtake from 'Fables'. Peter Buck: "I think we consciously put in as many chord changes as we possibly could. We can't play it without laughing." Working titles were 'The Fruity Song' and 'The Clever Ditty'. Splendidly inane pop, which would have cheered the album no end despite the cynicism of the lyrics. First released as the B-side of 'Can't Get There From Here'.

FEMME FATALE

Another Velvet Underground song, another outtake from 'Reckoning', recorded straight to two-track "the same hour as 'Pale Blue Eyes'". *Very* ragged, but still quite fun. First released as the B-side of 'Superman' (UK 12-inch).

WALTER'S THEME

Outtake from 'Reckoning': a brief but highly danceable jingle for Walter's Bar-B-Q, one of Peter's favourite Athens restaurants. Recorded late at night, while drunk.

KING OF THE ROAD

First released as the B-side of 'So. Central Rain'. From the same drunken session as 'Walter's Theme'. "If there was any justice in this world, Roger Miller should be able to sue for what we did to this song," Buck confessed. Actually, it's not bad. One yearns to hear their versions of other Miller classics, like 'England Swings'.

CHRONIC TOWN

With the CD release of 'Dead Letter Office' an extra five tracks were added, which had originally comprised 'Chronic Town', produced by Mitch Easter and R.E.M. and released as a 12" vinyl EP only on August 24, 1982 (IRS SP 70502). It would appear that Peter Buck had no hand in the remastering of this material. Mitch Easter, 1994: "I remember 'Chronic Town' completely fondly because it was so relaxed, and so open to cutting the tape up and putting pieces in backwards and stuff. And at the same time it was so non-business. There were some fireworks one night, so we went and sat on the roof for hours and watched the fireworks instead of working on the record – because we *could*, you know ? I mean, the set-up was technically really simple – I had almost nothing in the studio back then except a tape machine and a console and two compressors and one delay device. We couldn't *do* any fancy stuff."

Bill Berry : "A 'chronic town' is a city in the state of mind." It's also part of the lyric to 'Carnival'.

Jay Boberg of IRS, who signed R.E.M. on the strength of seeing one gig and hearing the tape of 'Chronic Town': "The thing that made me play the cassette again and again was that it kept getting better. It was not the kind of thing you listened to once or twice, casually, and said, 'Oh my God! This is tremendous!' It had a depth to it." 'Chronic Town' sold over 20,000 copies in its first year of release.

WOLVES, LOWER

Recorded last, as a last-minute replacement for 'Jazz Lips' (Easter: "a tone poem thing which was pretty funny". He's also described it as a "beat garbage dada thing") and 'Ages Of You'. This is the second version of the song they recorded (the first was too fast). Peter Buck: "Spooky gospel, that's what we wanted it to be."

Easter: "I was really big on all the noise junk that was on 'Wolves, Lower' – that middle section with the tape loop things and backwards whooshes and things – and I was really big on editing tape and putting takes together and stuff like that. And I think Michael liked that too, because it appealed to the sort of art school scene he was into at that time. What was so terrific about the 'Chronic Town' session was that they were absolutely open to all that stuff, and they thought it was fun, you know?"

Easter: "We did some of the vocals outside. There were a lot of bugs out there. Whenever that 'House in order' part comes up, I think you can hear tons of crickets. You don't really hear them, but they are there. You can kind of hear him say 'wolves' in a spoken voice and the spoken voice will sound different than the sung 'wolves'." According to one account, Easter even recorded Michael zipping and unzipping his flies.

Some think that this is about their relationship with Hib-Tone i.e. they're the wolves of the title, but the band are putting their "house in order". A wonderfully soaring harmonic chorus. This track was also given away as a flexi-disc with *Trouser Press* magazine in December 1982.

GARDENING AT NIGHT

One of their earliest original songs. Stipe has gone on record as saying that some people think the lyrics are "about my father, some people think they're about drugs, and some people think they're about gardening at night.

They're about all of them." Peter Buck has been more specific "There was an old guy in my neighbourhood who would be out gardening at 2 a.m. in his suit and tie. I'd see him when I was out trying to get beer at Magic

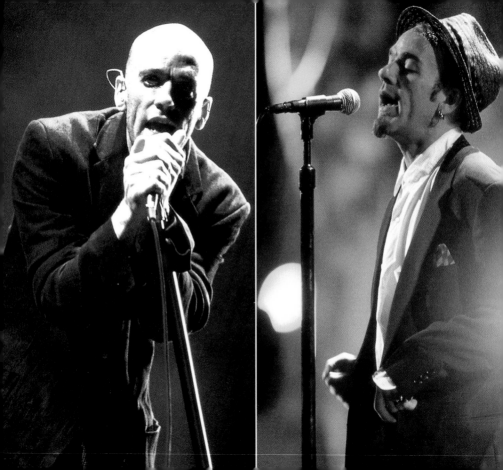

Mart or somewhere. I told Michael about the guy and he wrote the song." Which is fragile, ethereal and haunting folk-pop. The song also gave its name to the band's publishing company, Night Garden Music.

CARNIVAL OF SORTS (BOX CARS)

Lots of train imagery in this claustrophobic rocker, which kind of falls between two stools (or two tunes). Bill Berry hated this one.

1,000,000

Another one that can't make up its mind; a tinny rocker where half the time Stipe sounds like John Lydon, the other half like Donovan – and unsurprisingly the two halves don't really reconcile. "I could live a million years," he sings. Today, he probably feels like he already has.

STUMBLE

Low-grade folk-pop, with very odd (and jarring) drumming. The line about the APT refers to the Athens Party Line, an answerphone service run by Pylon's Michael Lachowski, which told callers where parties were being held that night.

In addition, the European 'IRS Years' version of this CD (IRS 0777 7 13199 2 1) contains two more tracks, though it's worth pointing out that Peter Buck had no hand in the selection of this material, and is almost certainly less than happy about it (see his comments in the Compilation Albums section under 'Best of R.E.M.').

GARDENING AT NIGHT (ACOUSTIC)

Tentative acoustic version, slow and weedy. According to IRS, an outtake from 'Reckoning', though it seems improbable they'd still be tinkering with it two albums on. Recorded straight to two-track.

ALL THE RIGHT FRIENDS

Great voodoo rockabilly workout, though a tad ragged (The Cramps would be proud of them). A previously unreleased song, recorded straight to two-track on 17/2/83.

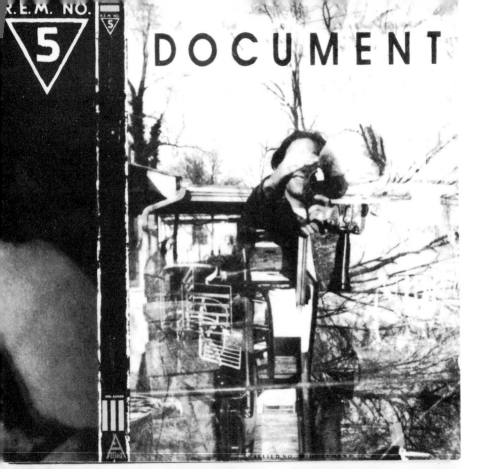

DOCUMENT

RELEASED SEPTEMBER 1987. CURRENT ISSUE: IRS DMIRG 1025

Though the experience of working with Don Gehman hadn't been ideal (he'd publicly expressed doubts that they'd ever have a hit single), R.E.M. still seem to have been keen to work with him again. This didn't happen, probably simply because Gehman wasn't available when R.E.M. needed to record one song ('Romance' – see 'Eponymous') for a movie soundtrack.

Ironically, Gehman suggested R.E.M. work with Scott Litt, thus rendering the question of who produced their next album redundant ("The biggest mistake of my life," Gehman later said). Though 'Romance' hadn't been their finest hour, the band really enjoyed working with Litt (who had also produced The dB's and Katrina and The Waves' superb 'Walkin' On Sunshine'), and invited him to co-produce their next album. It's a production partnership that has continued to this day.

Buck later explained why they hadn't used Gehman again: "The new songs, because of the way we wrote them, wouldn't have lent themselves to that big AOR thing."

But Gehman was pragmatic: "I felt that I was responsible for giving them a set of tools that worked for them. I showed them a method-ology of approaching a song, and production and sound, and they just took the next step. Scott has got a history of knowing exactly the same sort of stuff and, if anything, has got a more commercial background than I have."

Sessions commenced in March 1987 at the Nashville Sound Emporium, and was later mixed at Master Control in Los Angeles. Steve Berlin (of The Blasters and Los Lobos) provided horns. Scott Litt later confessed that one of their aims for the album had been to come up with songs that would get radio airplay. And why not? They'd waited long enough for it...

Litt admitted: "I like having a big sound. I like having bold sounds, and I like having a singer that grabs you. I wouldn't accept anything less." Whether it was Litt's influence, or whether Michael and the others were simply more confident after 'Lifes Rich Pageant', one of the most noticeable things about 'Document' was that the vocals were a lot clearer this time. Mike Mills: "We didn't set out to mix the vocals louder; it just seemed natural. There was a point where we sat back and listened to it and realised that the vocals were clearer and more out-front, but nobody had really noticed it or worried about it up to that point."

Which meant the lyrics were easier to make out, providing even more ammunition for the fanatics, otherwise known as the 'Distiples', as Stipe told Adrian Deevoy: "It's terrifying, really. They take my every utterance with deadly seriousness, even if I'm just drunk and talking a load of crap."

If it was crap (and it wasn't), at least it was fashionable – Stipe had become infatuated with chaos theory: "The whole album is about chaos. I've become very interested in chaos and the hypothesis that there is order within chaos, so I guess that kind of carried over into the recording." He also told *Musician* that "The whole album is about fire. About everything you think about fire as being cleansing, something that destroys everything in its path. It's an element

that's everywhere, the metaphorical and allegorical interpretations of 'Fire' are endless."

In the album's fire motif – and the fiery video for 'The One I Love' – some saw a reference to the Athens club Tyrone's, which had burned down in January 1982 ("The best club Athens has ever seen," said Mills). 'File Under Fire' read the note on the spine (echoing 'Reckoning') while the subtitle simply read: R.E.M. No. 5.

Working titles for the album included 'Mr Evil Breakfast', 'Lester Bangs' and 'Last Train To Disneyland/world' (Peter Buck: "To me, America in 1987 *is* Disneyworld.").

It was their first Top Twenty album, and their first million-seller. That month, they were on the cover of *Rolling Stone*, the headline reading simply: 'America's Best Rock 'n' Roll Band.' Their record contract with IRS had now been fulfilled, and they were up for grabs. They couldn't have been a more saleable item.

Miles Copeland, IRS Records, 1994: "After the fourth and fifth albums, they were getting to be a hot group and we went back to re-negotiate and said, 'We'd like to give you a lot of money right now and get two more records out of you.' Which is a traditional thing you do in this business. And they said, 'Well, no, we're happy. We don't need to re-negotiate, we don't need the money. We'll go through the contract and when we've delivered all the records we'll go to the open market, and obviously we'll consider IRS and we'll take it from there.'

"And they went to the open market and it ended up between IRS and Warner Bros, and then Warners said, 'Whatever IRS offer, we'll double it.' The offer was so huge I said to the group, 'If I were you, I'd take it. I can't even compete. They're offering you more money than my label's worth, and a higher royalty than my label is getting. So take the money and run.' So we shook hands and they went and did phenomenally well. And we continue to do very well on the catalogue, and we have a great relationship with them."

FINEST WORKSONG

Michael Stipe, 1987 : "In America, if you can't make money, they think it's because you're a failure. The work ethic is really intrinsic to American thought and that has a lot to do with the LP." Driving and anthemic, with wonderfully swooping bass, this seems to be both a call to political action and a comment on how the dignity of labour has been corrupted by greed and materialism (the Yuppies, in other words): "What we want and what we need has been confused."

WELCOME TO THE OCCUPATION

Folk-rock ballad that's almost a protest song ("listen to me"). It seems to be about cultural imperialism until the line "fire on the hemisphere below" implies that it's about American military intervention in Central America again. "The forest for the fire" could well be implying that we should be doing something about the rainforests. And we should.

EXHUMING McCARTHY

As in Senator Joe McCarthy, whose anti-Communist paranoia fuelled one of the most shameful periods in American history. It's also a dig at the Reagan administration (also prone to political witch hunts and anti-Communist hysteria).

Peter Buck: "It's the Eighties, and McCarthyism's coming back, so why not dig him up?" Introducing the song can be heard the tapping keys of Michael's typewriter (he was writing lyrics in the studio, just like Dylan used to). This veers from the jazzy (the sections where Mike sings "it's a sign of the times" – a nod to Prince?) to the bouncily poppy. Another hummable dig at capitalism, with a sampled extract of McCarthy being publicly humiliated.

DISTURBANCE AT THE HERON HOUSE

More elegant folk-rock. Michael thought this was "the most obvious song I've ever written, but not one person, not one, has worked out what in hell it's about." An *Animal Farm* type political fable? A call for animal liberation? I give up ...

STRANGE

Cover version of a Wire song. Gutsy rockout, with Stipe sounding a bit like John Lydon, Buck being very clever with his guitar and some wonderfully dumb beat group harmonies.

IT'S THE END OF THE WORLD AS WE KNOW IT (AND I FEEL FINE)

This is what Julie Burchill would call a 'shopping list' song (the kind of thing that Ian Dury used to excel at): a post-modern protest that owes more than a passing nod to Dylan's 'Subterranean Homesick Blues' (and is thus related to Chuck Berry's 'Too Much Monkey Business' and Elvis Costello's 'Pump It Up'). A joyous celebration of uncertainty at the end of the age, and not pessimistic in the least. Even Mike's plea "Time I had some time alone" sounds happy.

Supposedly, most of the lyrics were improvised in the studio; the last verse relates to a dream Stipe had, in which he was at a birthday party for the late Lester Bangs (the acerbic rock critic, whose writings have been posthumously collected as *Psychotic Reactions & Carburettor Dung*). Seeing that the other guests included Leonid Brezhnev, Lenny Bruce and Leonard Bernstein, Stipe realised that he was the only person present whose initials weren't 'L.B'. (in reality, Stipe and Buck had met Bangs at a party in New York in 1980).

Michael Stipe, 1987: "I wanted it to be the most bombastic vocal that I could possibly muster. Something that would completely overwhelm you and drip off your shoulders and stick in your hair like bubble gum." Chaos theory you can dance to.

THE ONE I LOVE

Verily, a hit; probably because most punters thought they were hearing a simple epic rock love song, i.e. they never bothered to listen to the words. Stipe thought it "better that they just think it's a love song at this point. That song just came up from somewhere, and I recognised it as being really violent and awful. But it wasn't directed at any one person. I would never ever write a song like that. Even if there was one person in the world thinking, 'This song is about me', I could never sing it or put it out."

Perhaps to emphasise that fact, Stipe's ex-girlfriend Caroline appears in the video.

He told *Musician* : "I've been announcing at shows that I wrote it to myself, because it's such an incredibly violent song, perhaps the most violent song I've ever written. It's very, very brutal. I almost didn't want to put it on the record. I thought it was too much. 'Harborcoat' and 'Laughing' were violent and brutal, but they're both so internal and folded in on themselves that no one would ever pick up on that except as a general gut feeling. 'The One I Love' is lyrically very straightforward. It's very clear that it's about using people over and over again. I think that's probably a sentiment everyone has felt at one time or another, so you can apply it to yourself. But it's not an attractive quality."

The working title was 'This One Goes Out'. Scott Litt bet Bill Berry that this would reach the Top Ten. He won.

FIREPLACE

Crazy world, crazy times; you might as well dance. And this mournful ballad is practically a waltz, were it not for the jazzy sax from Steve Berlin. More fire imagery, the lyrics inspired by a speech by Mother Ann Lee, the founder of The Shakers, a 17th Century celibate religious movement. Working title: 'The Swirly Song'.

LIGHTNIN' HOPKINS

Named after legendary bluesman Sam "Lightnin'" Hopkins, but it's not particularly bluesy – more R.E.M. go tribal, with heavy emphasis on percussion and a good deal of communal wordless moaning. Peter Buck: "I love Lightnin' Hopkins, and I've got hundreds of records by him. I had four with me the day we wrote 'Lightnin' Hopkins' on the 'Document' album. They were on a chair near Michael, and he improvised the words on the spot. If you listen closely it sounds like a screenplay about a black person, not necessarily Lightnin'. But with an inspiration like that, you don't want to mess with it. If it makes one kid check out a Lightnin' Hopkins record then it was worth doing." According to Buren Fowler, the Lightnin' Hopkins albums belonged to him.

KING OF BIRDS

Psychedelic sitar-like guitar, military-style drumming; this is evocative and folksy, in an Incredible String Band kind of way. Probably inspired by William Wharton's novel *Birdy*, which Stipe is known to have read belatedly in

1985 (the line on which the song fades, "everybody hit the ground" is a quote from the novel). "My kingdom for a voice" is a paraphrase of the famous speech from Shakespeare's *Richard III*.

ODDFELLOWS LOCAL 151

A slice of disturbingly jazzy story-telling that makes for very uneasy listening. Original title: 'Fire House'. Peter Buck, 1987: "There used to be Oddfellows Lodges all over town, just

like the Mooses or the Shriners. The song is actually about all these winos who used to live down the street from us. They used to live in cars. We call them the Motor Club. These old guys would sleep in the cars and drink all the time. I think there *was* a guy called Pee Wee as well. Michael knew them because he lived right next door to them. Every once in a while you'd give them five bucks or drop off a bottle." Michael also described the song as a "debunking of the myth-making of 'Fables Of The Reconstruction'."

The European 'IRS Years' CD version (0777 7 13200 2 6) contains an additional six tracks, all originally released as singles' B-sides:

FINEST WORKSONG (OTHER MIX)

First released as the B-side of the US 'Finest Worksong' 12-inch. Features added horns, but also sounds muted, slower and far less commercial.

LAST DATE

Gentle and pleasant countryish instrumental, a cover of a Floyd Cramer tune. Recorded on September 4, 1987, at John Keane's studio; first released as the B-side of 'It's The End Of The World As We Know It (And I Feel Fine)'.

THE ONE I LOVE

Live acoustic version. Poignant, mournful, wonderful. It sounds like Stipe is attempting to redeem the song's lyric by turning it into an apology – you half expect him to sing "I'm sorry" and turn it into 'So. Central Rain'. Recorded at McCabe's Guitar Shop in L.A. on May 24, 1987, and featuring Geoff Gans on second guitar. Gans – who worked for IRS as a sleeve designer on 'Eponymous' – had taped the show on a Walkman. First released as the B-side of 'The One I Love'.

TIME AFTER TIME ETC.

Slow and lengthy (and ramshackle) live version which segues into 'So. Central Rain' via a chunk of Peter Gabriel's 'Red Rain'. First released as the B-side of the 'Finest Worksong' 12-inch. Recorded in Utrecht, Holland, from a show broadcast by Vara Radio.

DISTURBANCE AT THE HERON HOUSE

Another live acoustic number from the McCabe's Guitar Shop show. It works pretty well acoustically (apart from a few fluffs in the solo), but makes the lyric sound even more bizarre. First released as the B-side of the UK 12-inch of 'The One I Love'.

FINEST WORKSONG (LENGTHY CLUB MIX)

First released as the B-side of the US 'Finest Worksong' 12-inch. Features horns, and the kind of self-indulgent mixing you only find on 1980s 12-inch B-sides. See also the section for 'Eponymous'.

GREEN

R.E.M.

GREEN

RELEASED NOVEMBER 1988. CURRENT ISSUE: WARNER BROTHERS 925 975-2

R.E.M. had signed to Warner Brothers for a five-album deal, allegedly for a ten million dollar advance. But money alone wasn't the reason for signing to a major. Warners had promised a high royalty, good planet-wide distribution (which IRS had never managed), and ownership of the masters would eventually revert to the group (allegedly after ten years). What's more – and this was certainly of paramount importance to them – they would continue to make music on their terms, retaining full artistic control. Lenny Waronker, Warners' president, stated that, "We understood the mentality of the band, and wouldn't pressure them to do certain things they couldn't do, aesthetically. We absolutely understood their aesthetic concerns. And at the same time wanted to get them as far as we could get them without interfering with that."

When asked why they'd signed to Warner Brothers, Stipe replied simply (and endearingly): "Bugs Bunny".

So they headed back to the studio, with co-producer Scott Litt. Or rather, two studios: Ardent Studios in Memphis and Bearsville Studios in Bearsville, New York. And they worked hard on their Warners début (Scott Litt described it as "the hardest effort I've put forth"). They experimented with swapping instruments (Bill Berry: "We've found a whole new songwriting technique now: just grab an instrument you don't know how to play, and fool around until it sounds right"), and with new instruments (mandolin and accordion). There was talk about making one side acoustic, one electric (remember when records had two sides?), but in the end there weren't enough acoustic numbers to make that idea viable.

Buck would later weary of journalists asking him to explain the album's title ("It's just a title. We could have called it 'Fred'"), but it was a lot snappier than the working title

('Think Tank Decoy') and it did carry resonance, implying solidarity with Green politics, a global consciousness and eco-awareness in general. It could also be taken as implying innocence and/or *naïveté*. As Stipe told *Rolling Stone*: "I decided that this had to be a record that was incredibly uplifting. Not necessarily happy, but a record that was uplifting to offset the store-bought cynicism and easy condemnation of the world we're living in now."

On another occasion he said: "'Document' for me was a very vitriolic statement. If this album is a reaction to 'Document', most of the songs that we wrote hopefully are very uplifting and that cynicism is passed over. I wanted to put hope into the music, and hopefully I did." One reason hope was important to them now was that they were in mourning: a note on the sleeve says "overseen by Curtis Goodman", referring to their long-time road manager, who had died of cancer the previous year.

And this début echoed another, Stipe confirmed to *Rolling Stone*: "For me, 'Green' had so many connections to 'Murmur'. It was very much in the back of my head the whole time we were working on it. From the album cover to the topics of the songs and the way the songs were carried out, to me, there's a great connection there." Recognising this closing of a circle, R.E.M. would feature 'Murmur' material live on the 'Green' tour (on at least one occasion playing it in its entirety) – they'd had to go and buy a copy of the record to re-learn the songs.

Not only was 'Green' spot on in mood for its time (consider how many "world leaders" lost their jobs in the following year), but it has a timeless quality that places it right up there with Van Morrison's 'Astral Weeks' and Love's 'Forever Changes' – it's a genuine classic. The later albums may have shifted more copies, but 'Green' is a more coherent work than any of them.

Of course, that doesn't mean it was commercially acceptable – something they'd known for a while. Scott Litt claims that early on in the recordings he started telling Warners: "Listen, I'd like to deliver you a record that's gonna sell 5,000,000 copies, but 'Green' is not that record." He was right, but it still outstripped 'Document', going straight into the US charts on release. But it peaked at number 15, and this must have been a far worse performance than Warners had hoped.

Its sales *may* have been harmed by the release of 'Eponymous', the 'greatest hits' package rushed out by IRS a month before (see the 'Compilation Albums' section for further details), but it's far more likely that the mass market just wasn't ready for R.E.M. yet (their turn would come).

But the critics were unanimously in favour. December saw R.E.M. on the cover of *Rolling Stone* once more, this time billed as 'America's Hippest Band', and the British press was even more ecstatic. *Q*'s Andy Gill called them "the best band in the world", and *Melody Maker*'s Allan Jones noted: "they could bow out now with 'Green' and we would remember them with nothing but awe." Amen.

POP SONG 89

"Should we talk about the weather? Should we talk about the government?" In other words, what's important? (It *could* be the weather). And what *is* the nature of pop music today, anyway? Stipe deflates all these questions by echoing The Doors' 'Hello, I Love You' and admitting he hasn't a clue as to the answers. "It's a complete piss-take," he's confessed. Great widdly-wop guitar, brooding organ, an infectious rhythm – this is almost commercial!

GET UP

Joyously bouncy pop, complete with Beatlish harmonies. Michael introduces this as "my favourite song" during *Tourfilm*. He's also said it's "a song about the fine line between the real and the fantastic." While he sings about dreams complicating his life, Mike Mills avows "Dreams they *complement* my life". Michael Stipe: "I think dreams are pretty crucial to everyone. Certainly to me, they're as real as anything else."

As he pointed out in 1990: "They're dumb words, but they're basically a call to action: 'Get off your ass! Do something! Do anything! Get a life! You're going to be around for another maybe sixty years. Get up and do something!'"

The music boxes featured here came at the request of Bill Berry, who'd had a dream about twelve music boxes playing; with due regard for synchronicity, these were duly bought and taped.

YOU ARE THE EVERYTHING

Bill Berry: "Peter came up with the mandolin line for that. I picked up the bass, and Mike picked up the accordion, and in about twenty minutes we had the song."

Heartbreakingly beautiful, with a serenity that echoes its lyrics, and (one feels) naked honesty. A mystical, evocative, affirmative hymn – to life, to a beautiful woman, to music, to everyday contentment at its most sublime, to the Beyond. This may well be R.E.M.'s finest moment.

STAND

Deeply profound or profoundly dumb (probably both) bouncy pop, featuring a brand new wah-wah pedal Peter had bought that day (he'd never even played one before). Michael's friend Georgina Falzarano claims this song was inspired by her terrible sense of direction: "The left/right thing is very difficult for me. Michael was really intrigued with how I remember direction and asked me exactly what it was I do. I told him I visualise I'm standing in front of my house, because when I'm looking at my house I can tell that's north, then I can tell where east

and west and south are in relationship to where I am." R.E.M. allowed this to be used as the theme tune to the appropriately titled American TV show *Get A Life.*.

WORLD LEADER PRETEND

The first (and so far, only) R.E.M. song to have its lyrics included in the sleeve packaging, an indication of how much Michael wanted to get his message across, as an 'Everyman' figure. Michael Stipe: "Something I was really stressing on 'Green' was that the individual has a great power and a great strength. People have to realise that, to tap it. 'World Leader Pretend' is exactly about that: you have to overcome yourself before you can overcome what's outside of yourself."

The song is thus more about personal/spiritual growth than about Eastern Europe (for example); on a personal level, it could be interpreted that Stipe was keen on shattering his image. But as he told *Q,*: "I know what I'm doing. I recognise when that caricature is getting out of hand and I pull back, and I recognise when it needs to go further and I push it."

He's also described the line "Let my machine talk to me" as being "the turning point of the entire song, where it is very clear to me that the machine is the reptile brain, or in Jungian terms, the feminine side coming through and overwhelming the masculine, making the person in the song completely whole." This track also features cellist Jane Scarpantoni and pedal steel guitarist Bucky Baxter.

THE WRONG CHILD

Mournful mandolin-based folk-rock. The song was supposedly inspired by a newspaper article about the experience of a burns victim going out in public for the first time ("I'm not supposed to be like this, but it's okay"). Michael: "I know a lot of people who are physically handicapped. It just sort of came to me."

ORANGE CRUSH

Subversive anthemic rock: this is *not* about a soft drink (as Michael sometimes liked to con people), but about Agent Orange, the defoliant deployed by the US ("agents of the free") in the Vietnam War which had horrific long-term biological effects on both Vietnamese civilians and US troops. Which explains all the helicopter noises...

Stipe's father had served in Vietnam, but in 1989 Peter Buck denied that Michael had any personal axe to grind: "He *didn't* write it about his father. His father was in the helicopter corps. I'm not sure if he actually dropped the stuff, but he was around it. Even so, the song's not about his father's life, though his father sometimes thinks it is."

Mitch Easter, 1994: "'Orange Crush' was really mechanical and probably done a lot on a Fairlight or something. If I had suggested that on the 'Murmur' sessions they'd have shot me on the spot, and that would've been the end of it."

TURN YOU INSIDE OUT

Neil Young influenced guitar attack! Not about personal relationships, (except perhaps as a metaphor for political ones), but about fandom, and about how performers – political as well as pop – can manipulate an audience. Just say no, this seems to be saying – or at least, use a bit of discrimination ("divide your culture, pearls and paste"). In *Tourfilm* Stipe dedicates the song to the Exxon Corporation, at that time responsible for a massive oil spill in Alaska, but that would seem to be unrelated to this (though still a justifiable rant). Recorded during the mixing stages, in Woodstock. Percussion by Keith LeBlanc.

HAIRSHIRT

More mournful folk-rock ("I'm so alone"), but still optimistic and exquisitely done. "Carbon black" is used in ink, but the use of it in context would seem to relate to Carbon-14 testing of bones to date them. About penance/redemption, or dogs, or both. During the 'Green' tour, Michael did indeed swing his megaphone on stage.

Scott Litt: "'Hairshirt' started out as just a couple of chords on a mandolin or a piano. Michael would take that tape and come up with the whole verse and chorus, and then we would add the instrumentation after the vocals were done. This was a marked departure from their previous writing. Instead of doing the vocals last, they started doing the vocals first."

Peter Buck: "Michael said, 'Play that for six minutes. I've got enough for six minutes.' So we got a clock out and did just that." Bill Berry apparently hates this one.

I REMEMBER CALIFORNIA

Doomily impressionistic shopping list of images connected with the "edge of the continent" that manages to make even fruit and sunshine and California girls sound depressing. The least accessible track on the album.

Michael Stipe, 1989: "The music and the words really capture for me everything that Southern California is. I have this whole theory that people move west until they get to the end of the continent, when they can't move anymore, so they essentially set up a lemming camp. Rather than jump into the ocean, they created Los Angeles." In 1994 he admitted, "I just despise the way my voice sounds on that."

(UNTITLED)

After the doom 'n' gloom of the last track, they wind up the album with a final blast of ethereal beauty and hope: a song about love and staying up late. Credited as 'The Eleventh Untitled Song' when released as a B-side to 'Stand', this features Peter Buck on drums: "Bill says it's impossible to play that drum part. Not that it's hard, just that it's so bad it's impossible to play perfectly all the way through. It's one thing to make a mistake like that, but it's another to do it on purpose for four minutes."

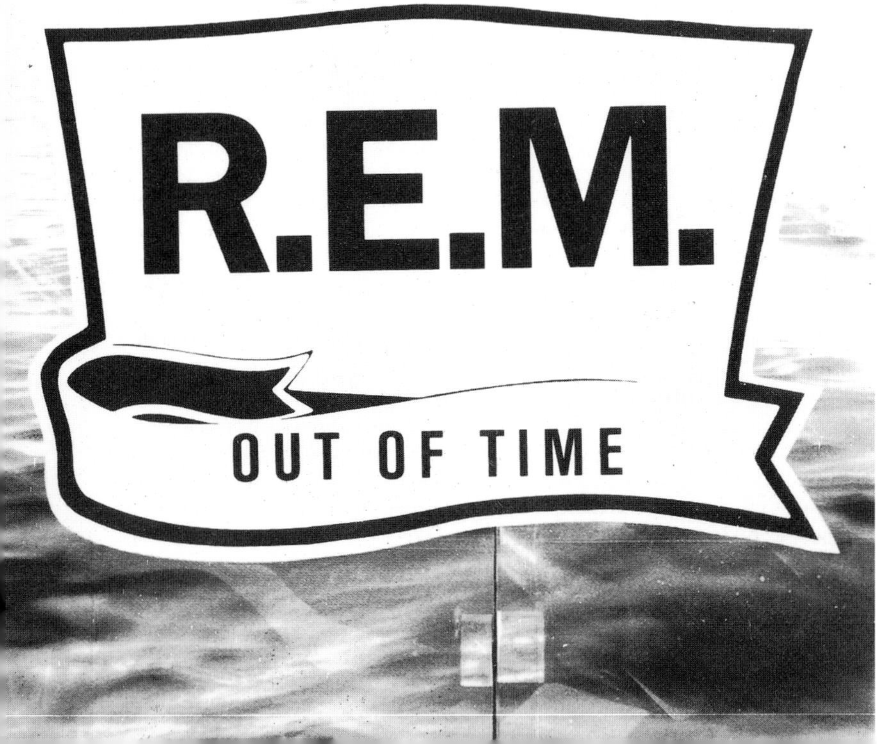
R.E.M.
OUT OF TIME

OUT OF TIME

RELEASED MARCH 1991. CURRENT ISSUE: WARNER BROTHERS 7599-26496-2

The Green tour had been gruelling beyond belief (see section on *Tourfilm*); perhaps that's why they deliberately recorded a follow-up with instrumentation that would make it difficult (if not impossible) to play live. As Peter Buck put it: "We really felt the last tour was a kind of peak, playing the biggest places we ever played. I thought we did it better than 99 per cent of the people that play arenas. It was a good show. But if we were to do it again this year, it would just be the same thing. For our own sanity we thought it would be a good idea to take time off. I don't know what the next step is: we're going to make records, we're going to be a band, you know."

They were all – Michael in particular – tired of the pressures of the road, as Bill Berry summed up: "We pretty much got burned out. As much fun as touring has been for us over the years, that one really was like, *Whoa!* A little more than we thought it would be. Michael was really affected by it, more than the rest of us. He requested that we not tour with this record, and we were all, like, 'yeah, that's a great idea'. I mean, how do you eclipse what we just did? Also, it allows us to get back in and do another record pretty quickly. " And with no impending tour built into their itinerary, for once R.E.M. could take their time in the studio.

In fact, the record came together more quickly than anyone could have predicted, largely because of the workaholic nature of the parties involved. Peter Buck: "After the 'Green' tour, we were not even supposed to talk to each other in 1990 until the end of March/beginning of April. Basically, we'd been together for two years straight, with the record, rehearsals, then touring. So we said, 'Let's get away, we need to get some time apart.' And we ended up rehearsing on January 6. That's just what we do. We'd be at a party and say, 'You know, maybe we should play a little bit.' Bill, Mike and I turned out about ten new songs in two weeks."

Bill Berry: "We wrote songs for the album off and on between January and July of 1990. It's not really like going back to work, to come down here and meet for five minutes and decide if we feel like working. We made ourselves come down here every day during the week and at least go in and play around for a little bit. If we didn't feel like anything was happening, we'd break and go get a beer. But if anything was going on, we'd stick with it till we came up with something. The trick is showing up. If you show up often enough, something will come out."

Since they had the time to experiment, they did so. Bill Berry: "The success of 'Green' literally afforded us the time to not have to hurry through it, to take our time. If things didn't work, we'd start again." The results startled Michael Stipe when he first heard them: "I stayed away for a month and a half and let them get to it. And when I came in, they had this group of songs that were unlike anything I'd heard from R.E.M. It was classic R.E.M., but the instrumentation was skewered, completely different from what we'd done in the past."

For the first time, they would use guest stars (including rapper KRS-1 of Boogie Down Productions and Kate Pierson of Athens pioneers The B-52's). In addition, Peter Holsapple – who had been added to their ranks for the 'Green' tour – played on over half the album, fuelling speculation that he was formally joining the group.

Peter Buck: "It helps me knowing there's someone who'll play the riffs along with me so I can play something else. My goal is to record my parts strictly live and never do any overdubs. We apportioned the parts so that six of the seven songs Peter Holsapple's on, I play the live instrument – the mandolin, for example – right into a microphone. I'd like to do the next record totally live with side musicians. I like the idea of a performance."

And they were using strings, more lavishly than they'd ever done before. Peter Buck: "I'd been pushing to do a string-laden record for years. I like baroque-sounding records. I think it helped that we were on the road a whole year, because we were so sick of electric guitars, drums and bass that when we started rehearsing we wrote everything on other instruments. When we hired the string arranger, we told him what we were looking for: a four-to-eight person string section, lots of cellos – kind of stark. We didn't want it syrupy. We had it pretty seriously arranged by the time we began recording – it's the most finished album we've done as far as going in with ideas is concerned. The demos were pretty concrete."

The string arranger was Mark Bingham, who had worked with Michael Stipe on the superb Disney tribute album 'Stay Awake'. Bingham brought in nine members of the Atlanta Symphony Orchestra. Also on board was New Orleans horn player Kidd Jordan, and John Keane on pedal steel guitar. And the songs themselves were radically different. Bill Berry: "This is the first time we actually wrote a body of songs around the keyboard. Mike was always playing bass a lot as a result. Peter really did not want to have a guitar-oriented record, so he found himself playing mandolin a lot, just to keep it fresh and fun. Most of the songs were written with me on bass, Pete on mandolin and Mike on the keyboards. I equate keyboards with strings – the way you can work with them in the context of a song – so the amount of strings on the record was really a natural thing, because they pretty much echoed the keyboard part."

For Michael Stipe, lyrically this would be "a record of challenges. A lot of them are real clear-cut. (1) I would write love songs; (2) they would not be political songs; and (3) I would use the first person singular instead of the third plural. I felt I'd pushed the third person as far as I could on 'Lifes Rich Pageant' and 'Document'. Everything was sounding anthemic, because we were saying 'we' all the time instead of 'I' or 'me' or 'you'. With this record I wanted to move toward more of a personal politic."

But personal doesn't automatically mean autobiographical, and it's worth bearing in mind that the working title for 'Out Of Time' was 'Fiction'; as Michael pointed out: "To the world and to my audience, I'd like to say here and now that when I sing 'I' in a song, that doesn't necessarily mean 'Michael Stipe, the singer'. It means I'm taking a lot of creative liberties with the idea of writing characters and, as a lyricist, trying to hurl myself into situations I may or may not have ever been in before. *When* I write an autobiographical record, I guarantee you'll know it – it'll be loud and clear!"

He also said: "I've never written an out-right love song, and I'm not sure that of the eleven songs on this record I've written an outright love song, but I'm trying. The record is about love and it's about memory and it's about time. Those are three things that for me as a songwriter are pretty new territory."

Robyn Hitchcock (on many of whose records Peter Buck had played) told *Mojo* about the group's writing technique: "They record about 40 chord sequences and then Michael comes in with his notebook, writes words for about half of them and they throw out the rest. There's a very high casualty rate. But there's a lot of advantages to working this way. For example, Mike and Peter wrote 'Shiny Happy People' – Mike wrote the chords on an acoustic, Peter did the electric guitar embroidery. But one songwriter alone, writing the chords, mightn't have imagined Peter's guitar or the kind of lyrics Michael came up with. In fact, Michael took the track away and turned up later saying, 'It's called 'Shiny Happy People', and it goes like this!' And Mike said, 'You can't *possibly* call it 'Shiny Happy People'! What kind of title is that?' And he had to admit eventually that Michael was right."

Sessions began at Bearsville Studios in Woodstock in September 1990, later moving to John Keane's Athens Studio for overdubbing. Mixing took place at Prince's Paisley Park Studios that December. Many of the basic tracks were recorded live, with few overdubs other than vocals.

Of the finished record, Mike Mills thought that it "very definitely is going to require a few listens", adding bemusedly, "I don't know what people are going to make of this album." But Bill Berry was more confident. "It's the record we've always wanted to make," he said simply.

The album title came about when the final deadline for Warners to know the album's title came around. After debating the merits of dozens of titles (among them were: 'Fiction', 'Cat Butt', 'Love And Squalor' [after J.D. Salinger's *For Esme, With Love And Squalor*], 'Borehole' and 'Imitation Crab Meat') the band had failed to agree on anything they all liked, but the choice couldn't be put off any longer. "We're out of time," Mills told the others. And lo, it came to pass...

Though Warners were allegedly frustrated that the group would not be touring to promote the album (what century are *they* living in?), comfort came in the fact that the group had finally actively embraced the possibilities of promotional videos (see the entry for *This Film Is On* in the 'Videos' section).

And this paid off. In September 1991, R.E.M. were nominated for nine categories in the MTV awards. They won six of them. The following February they picked up two Grammy Awards. Stipe took these TV opportunities to wear T-shirts and a baseball cap bearing slogans dear to his heart: 'Rainforest', 'Love Knows No Colours', 'Wear A Condom', 'Choice', 'Alternative Energy Now', 'The Right To Vote', 'Handgun Control Now' and 'White House Stop AIDS'. Perhaps he simply wanted to assure people that all these love songs *didn't* mean that he had abandoned social concerns entirely.

But the love songs served them well. 'Out Of Time' is, quite simply, a marvellous pop record. It went to Number 1 in the US, and sold six million copies in its first year of release. In fact, 'Out Of Time' went to Number 1 around the globe: the States, England, Italy, Greece, Israel... Peter Buck noted : "It's really strange, because we'd never sold that many records overseas, and all of a sudden we're going gold in Chile, platinum in Brazil – that kind of odd feeling of being huge in a place we've never been."

But if the world wanted to see them, they now felt a lot differently about seeing the world. "The actual performing is usually a joy," said Stipe in '92. "The difficult part is getting from place to place and trying to maintain some base of reality. That's difficult. It's a very bizarre way to travel. Sometimes you realise that you've flown halfway around the world to sing 18 songs. That's such a weird thing."

Bill Berry echoed him: "We used to be a live band that stopped off in the studio every 15 months. But the priorities are changing." And those priorities did *not* include touring.

RADIO SONG

Michael Stipe: "I hope people have enough of a sense of humour to realise I'm kind of taking a piss at everyone, myself included. Hopefully, they'll get the humourous intent of the song, with my opening plea about the world collapsing and KRS-One's closing rap, which I find really funny and thought-provoking."

With a style that veers from street boogie to epic string-laden ballad, this takes a scalpel to the medium and its place in our lives. Bill Berry, 1991: "We don't owe radio shit. Commercial radio never wanted to play us, but we sneaked through the cracks just because we had a fan base that couldn't be denied. It's not like we're biting the hand that's feeding us; it's more like we're biting the hand that's dicking us around."

Peter Buck on rap music: "It's like everything else. Ninety five per cent of it is shit and the other five per cent of it is great."

fairly well-written obsession song that was widely misinterpreted... I was trying to write 'Every Breath You Take'. Is that embarrassing? I don't think so. It's a great song; I was trying to write a better one." Supposedly the title is a Southern expression meaning to be "at your wit's end," or "at the end of your rope." Was this romance related to depression? Who knew? But Buck told *The Independent* that he thought the song was autobiographical.

Peter Buck: "That's totally live – acoustic guitar, bass, mandolin and drums. No overdubs, no changes. Mike put down the string part."

LOSING MY RELIGION

Mandolin kicks off this song of loss and confusion, riddled with spiritual/romantic desperation. Michael Stipe admitted that it "could be a comment on the state of the world, very easily. In fact, it's an extension of 'World Leader Pretend'." He also called it a "song of unrequited love".

Not that anybody else saw it that way, and many of the more po-faced religious-minded took offence. Stipe later dismissed these views, calling the song "nothing more than a

LOW

An old song that had been tested out live; bass and organ-dominated. Seems to be about manic depression ("howling at the moon/morning finds me laughing"), with its talk of highs and lows. Then again, that also sounds just like love. Michael Stipe: "It's just a song. It was written on the road, and I put together a bunch of nonsense phrases. I never meditated on it, it is as I wrote in a feverish moment somewhere touring around the world. I think it's kinda funny, actually." Referring to the line, "I skipped the part about love," he said, "That's how I always felt about love songs, about pop music. It was like, 'Get them out of my face !' They're all so horrible and manipulative.'" Michael's vocal is the original 'scratch' vocal (normally only a guide for himself later on) laid down while the band were recording rhythm tracks.

NEAR WILD HEAVEN

The Beach Boys meet The Fifth Dimension, and go to the country. Elegantly crafted pop song, a giant leap from anything you could have predicted of them previously. Lyrics by Mike Mills, supposedly.

ENDGAME

Almost an instrumental, but for Mills and Stipe la-la-la-ing over the top of it. "Endgame" is a chess term, also a Samuel Beckett play... This has echoes of Mason Williams, The Beatles' 'Sun King', and – I think David Cavanagh was the first to point this out – the instrumentals on Nick Drake's *Bryter Layter*, which is an essential purchase if you don't own one yet.

SHINY HAPPY PEOPLE

The Mamas & Papas live! Probably the most upfront, no-nonsense pop song in the entire R.E.M. catalogue, kicked into another dimension by the presence of Kate Pierson and the three-way vocal harmony. Peter described it as being "so relentlessly upbeat you want to throw up. Sometimes you can revel in a little bit of *naïveté*, and that's just me and Michael's little wish."

Michael Stipe: "The last thing I wanted to do was write a song that was ostensibly happy but very tongue-in-cheek. I just don't want to be a cynical person at all. There are elements of cynicism in myself I'm sure trickle through, but I just don't think this is a time for cynicism. It's too easy to say the world is a mess and I don't give a shit and why even bother? That's why I think music like this is so important. It's not a diversion tactic, it's not a distraction from the world at large, but it is a sign of hope, and I say that with no irony."

Criticised for writing this rather than airing his views on, say, the global political situation, Stipe responded: "With everything that's going on on a global level right now, a song that will make people happy, and lift them out of the general melée of the world, is not a bad thing. Maybe we can help turn the tide a little bit with a really good, really positive, really happy song." Hear, hear.

Of the tricky time changes, Bill Berry admitted: "We tried over and over to get the parts to fit together right, and in the end I still don't think we nailed it exactly."

vein. Michael Stipe: "This is about someone who thinks they're in love, but they're probably not." He also said that it "doesn't make sense to anybody but me. It's a complete fabrication, but there's something there." Featuring Mills' distinctive yodel, a harpsichord and a lyrical steal from John Keats' 'Ode To A Nightingale.'

BELONG

The spoken word vocals were recorded by Michael on a Walkman in his garage. He later said that it was about "a mother and child, especially the strong bond that exists between them. The voice is neither hers nor the child's, however. It's someone else commenting on the sense that the bond between a mother and child is the most powerful love of all."

The refrain makes the whole thing sound like a joyous Native American chant, gatecrashed by beatniks with a piano and a stand-up bass. I love it to bits.

HALF A WORLD AWAY

More baroque pop, again in the epic love song

TEXARKANA

Countryish rocker, named after the town on the Texas/Arkansas border (Bill Berry: "It's a beautiful place, but you wouldn't go there for enlightenment"), with the string section keeping up the 'epic' feel. Most of the lyrics were written by Mike Mills, supposedly. John Keane on pedal steel guitar.

COUNTRY FEEDBACK

Michael Stipe: "That's a demo tape we did prior to making the record. We liked it so much, we left it like it is. My vocal is the first and only time I sang that song. In fact, when I went in to sing it, it wasn't even a song. I had a number of quatrains on a piece of paper, and I just started singing. It was like a projectile-vomiting cathar-sis. The next day I came back and listened to it, and by golly, it was a pretty powerful song."

Peter Buck: "We didn't have a song. I walked in, I had four chords. I put them down with Bill playing bass. I put the feedback on it. John Keane put the pedal steel on it. Michael walked in and said, 'Oh, I've got words for that.' The next day he just sang it. The total recording time, not including the mix, was, like, 35 minutes. It's really nice if you can get it to flow like that." Buck also revealed that: "Usually, (Michael) has pretty concise words. We get to look them over. With 'Country Feedback', he just had two little drawings on a piece of paper – an Indian head and an arrow, I think – and he just kind of shouted."

Michael : "It's a love song, but it's certainly from the uglier side. It's pretty much about hav-ing given up on a relationship." He's also called it his "favourite R.E.M. song on record." Slow, and reminiscent of Neil Young brooding about something painful, this is, as David Cavanagh has rightly pointed out, a country song with feedback. Don't you just love R.E.M.'s simplici-ty when it comes to song titles?

ME IN HONEY

Michael Stipe: "Specifically, that song to me is an answer to 10,000 Maniacs' 'Eat For Two'. It's a male perspective on pregnancy, which I don't think has really been dealt with. There's a real push me/pull you issue, saying 'I had noth-ing to do with it', yet on the other hand saying, 'Wait – I have feelings about this'." Kate Pierson yodels over a driving rhythm introduc-tion, then Stipe comes in to yell his pain over what I'd call a raga if Spinal Tap hadn't killed off the word forever. This time the beatniks have gatecrashed a skiffle group: the results – and this whole album – raised the standards of modern pop music, and of what it could achieve when it really tried.

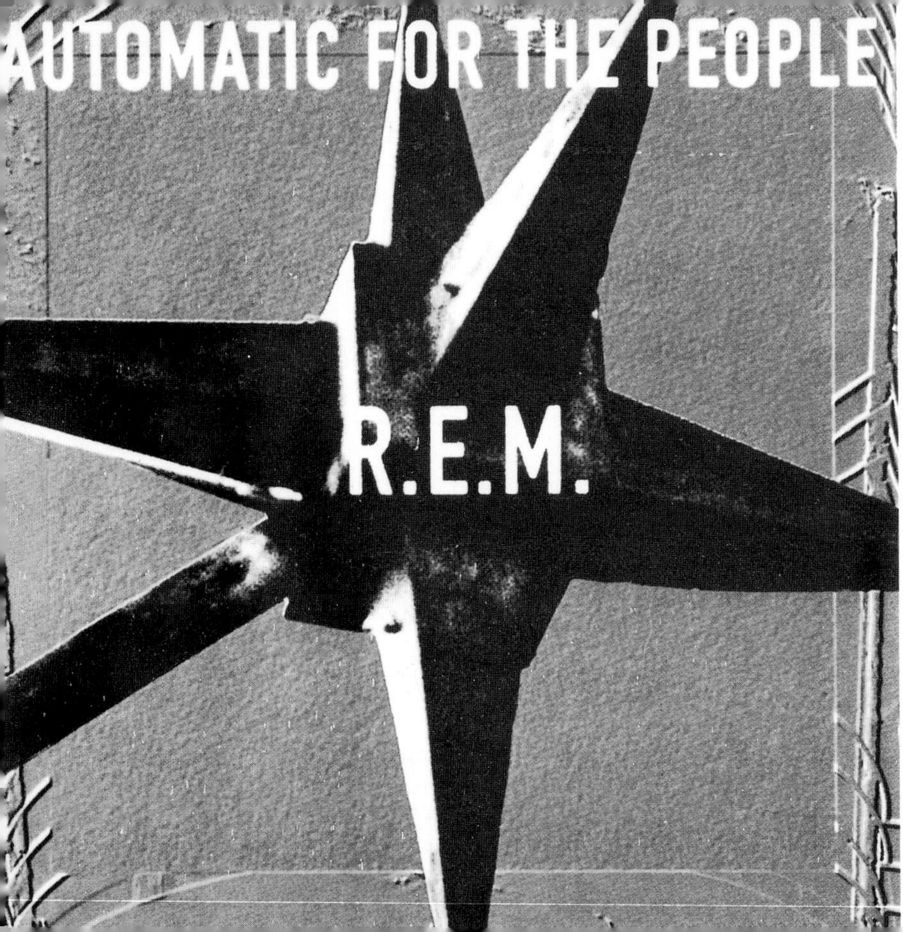
AUTOMATIC FOR THE PEOPLE
R.E.M.

AUTOMATIC FOR THE PEOPLE

RELEASED: OCTOBER 1992. CURRENT ISSUE: WARNER BROTHERS 9362-45055-2

"**N**ormally people who sell nine to ten million albums, you don't hear from them for four years," Peter Buck commented, explaining the fact that this was something the workaholic R.E.M. wanted to avoid. In fact, Mills, Buck and Berry were back in John Keane's Athens studio demoing new songs with Scott Litt mere months after the release of 'Out Of Time'. This time, however, they were minus Peter Holsapple. The guitarist – supposedly unhappy about his status as a hired hand who earned a wage rather than a percentage and who remained excluded from the songwriting process – quit to record an album with his former dBs partner Chris Starney called Mavericks .

Peter Buck: "Things happen – you sell a lot of records and things get weird. It just isn't easy being the fifth member of our band. No one else is going to write songs with us. It's a closed shop and it's tough to deal with. I wouldn't want to be in a band where I didn't have input in the songwriting or arrangements and stuff. I wish money would have nothing to do with this. We played for free together for so long that it's a shame to have business things get in between us. But on the other hand, we write the songs, we're the band. It's fucked in a way, but we're not going to open it up. It's not a monetary thing; it's just the way that we are."

Holsapple's lips remain sealed on the matter, probably for contractual reasons.

But he was enthusiastic about the new songs. Though the original intention had been to do a rock guitar album (i.e. something they could play live more easily than the 'Out Of Time' material), things weren't turning out that way, and he didn't seem to mind. "We'll have a folk-rock orchestra album," Buck told *Spin* magazine early on in the sessions. "The stuff is all turning out different. We've got a bunch of weird kind of Arabic folk songs."

If anything, the results would be even quieter than the previous album, the strings more

lavish – in fact, "folk-rock orchestra" is a pretty good description. "We thought it was going to be a live-sounding rock album," Buck said after the album was completed. "But halfway through we realised it was going to be quiet and droney, so that's what we went with." Former Led Zeppelin bassist and keyboard player John Paul Jones provided string arrangements for four songs ('Drive',

'Everybody Hurts', 'The Sidewinder Sleeps Tonight' and 'Nightswimming'). "I was really impressed with how melodic and non-saccharine his arrangements were," said Buck. Thirteen orchestral musicians are credited on the sleeve, under the conductorship of George Hanson. Originally, half the songs were to be drumless.

Once demos were complete, Stipe joined the others at Daniel Lanois' Kingsway studios in New Orleans. Recording continued at Bearsville in New York State, then Criteria in Miami, and Bosstown in Atlanta. The album was finally mixed at Heart's Bad Animals Studio in Seattle. All of this studio-hopping probably had a lot more to do with seeing a bit of the country than with anything technical.

This time the lyrics again seemed to concern personal matters, notably death and mourning. "I'm in the process of depoliticising myself," Michael Stipe later told *Rolling Stone*. "I'm glad that people look at the band as politically active. I think that's healthy. But it's a lot to carry, and to quote myself, not everyone can carry the weight of the world. It's enough that people know that R.E.M. are thinking, compassionate people – human beings who support a number of causes, publicly and privately. I don't have to jump on top of a building and scream. I'm not a very good speaker – that's the end – all of it." But as he'd said at the time of 'Out Of Time': "I'm not saying that I will never write another political song – in fact, I think even though thematically this record is love songs, there's a great deal of politics involved

and they're not just personal politics."

But Stipe's public solidarity with AIDS awareness – coupled with his gaunt appearance, his reluctance to appear in videos, the references to death on the record and the fact that the gay community *wanted* to believe he was gay, whatever he said (or didn't say) on the subject – fuelled rumours that Stipe himself was suffering from AIDS. It was one of rock's more bizarre rumours (Paul is dead!), which took a while to dissipate.

But as Peter Buck pointed out: "Michael is one of the few writers I can think of who can actually write songs about friendship and stuff. You don't know who he's singing to or whether there's a sexual relationship involved." As to the media focus on Michael's personal life, Buck said that Stipe was (quite understandably): "just sick of it. The band are asked about guitar effects, but journalists want to talk to Michael about his childhood".

And anyway – though the media still find it hard to accept – R.E.M. has four voices, not one. And in the songwriting process, Michael doesn't necessarily write *all* the lyrics. As Buck told *Q*: "On every record there's one of us who has less of an involvement than maybe the next record, but nobody needs to know that. By the time we write the bridges and intros and rewrite stuff, it's all of ours anyway. Since we split the money equally, there's no real reason to get egotistical about it. Saying who wrote what is counterproductive, like family business. I like the idea of the four of us indivisible; you can't drive a wedge between us. That's how we stay together."

The album took its title from a sign in a favourite diner, Weaver D's Fine Foods in Clarke County, Georgia, which read : "Delicious Fine Foods. Automatic For The People." The owner Dexter Weaver was approached for permission to use the slogan by Peter and Michael, and he told them the saying meant: "Ready, Quick and Efficient". And Michael said, "Woo, that's what we are". Within weeks of the album's release the sign was stolen by over-zealous R.E.M. fans who later returned it with $10 and a note of apology. Yup, sounds like R.E.M. fans.

Dexter Weaver: "Vice President Al Gore was here in Athens campaigning at the Tate Center over the University of Georgia, and Michael introduced him at the rally. Gore said Bush and Quayle was 'Out Of Time', but him and Bill Clinton was going to be 'Automatic For The People'. I wasn't there, but everywhere I went that night in town, people were telling me that Al Gore used my slogan. That's great, because we need a President who is going to be 'For The People'."

The success of 'Out Of Time' had evidently done wonders for their self-confidence. 'Automatic For The People' is an assured, mature work that combines polished production with polished performance and some of their best songs to date. It went straight in at Number 2 in the US, Number 1 in the U.K. It's now sold over 14 million copies world-wide.

DRIVE

"Smack, crack, bushwhacked," are the album's opening words, referring either to the increase of street drugs and resultant violence, or to the state of the nation under George Bush, or an optimistic prophecy of his defeat. Or all three. (Four years earlier, Michael Stipe had placed a pro-Dukakis ad in an Athens student newspaper, urging people to vote Democratic with the phrase: "Don't get Bushwacked."). There are echoes of

David Essex's 'Rock On' (though Essex was himself echoing Leon Russell). Broodingly atmospheric (and far from cheerful), with echoing vocals and booming bass set against delicate guitar and tasteful strings. Heck of a choice for a single, though.

TRY NOT TO BREATHE

Another of Stipe's "vomit songs" i.e. written quickly, in one sitting. A message from an old man, tired of his life but still clinging to it. This doesn't sound like *anybody* else in pop, ancient or modern.

THE SIDEWINDER SLEEPS TONIGHT

The album's first vaguely happy track – real bouncy pop, with gorgeously sweeping strings. The title obviously references 'The Lion Sleeps Tonight', as does the opening yodel. They'd actually recorded that song as well (it surfaced as a B-side – see the entry for 'The Automatic Box' in the 'Compilation Albums' section), so that may have been the jumping off point for this. Peter Buck: "Don't ask me what that's about. Part of it is trying to get into somebody's apartment to spend the night. The rest of it is just whatever Michael wanted to say. There are some things I just don't worry about. That's one of them." A sidewinder is a small rattlesnake. The lyric includes the kind of shopping list you'd imagine Stipe making in reality: can of beans, Dr. Seuss book, falling star ... Where do you *buy* falling stars, anyway ?

EVERYBODY HURTS

An anti-suicide song, with lots of good advice – "hold on", "take comfort in your friends". The tastefulness of the arrangement mirrors the economy of the lyric; the song may have been aimed at teenagers, but it's proof of R.E.M.'s maturity. Peter Buck: 'Everybody Hurts' is like a soul ballad. If Otis Redding were alive I bet he'd have covered it."

Peter Buck: "If you ask Michael, he'll say that not one of the songs is about himself. I know that's bullshit. On 'Everybody Hurts' there was a line that went: 'When everything is wrong, everybody hurts, even the singer of the song'. But in the end he said, 'I'm not going to sing that'."

Mike Mills: "He came up with the lyrics in the time it took us to go through the song three or four times. None of us really thought it would see the light of day. It was kind of a joke song at first. But Michael, in my opinion, is the best lyricist alive, and that song's a great example of how he polished a turd."

Peter Buck: "I guess people think when Michael's being obscure it's because he can't express himself. In fact, he's trying to find another way to say things in a way that's real to him, that isn't a cliché. He wanted that particular song to reach teenagers and not be misunderstood. You don't want something that needs a Maths degree to go through when you're trying to reach a 17-year-old and say, 'It's OK – things are tough but they get better.' There's not a line out of place in there."

NEW ORLEANS INSTRUMENTAL No. 1

So titled presumably because that's where it was recorded. Unlike most of the instrumentals from this period that turned up as B-sides (see the 'Automatic Box' entry again), this one has a tune: jazz-folk, with a bit of psychedelia

round the edges. It reminds me of the instrumentals on the Mamas and Papas' 'Deliver', but that's probably just me.

SWEETNESS FOLLOWS

A song of grief, and of coming of age. Losing a close relative is like joining a club: if you've been through it, you know what it's like; if you haven't, you don't. From the sound of it, R.E.M. do. Poignant folk-psychedelia featuring cello by Knox Chandler, making it sound reminiscent of The Beatles' 'Eleanor Rigby'.

MONTY GOT A RAW DEAL

"Nonsense isn't new to me," sings Stipe (accurately), and I for one have no idea what this is about. Sounds almost like a traditional folk song, and again features cello by Knox Chandler.

IGNORELAND

Overtly political rocker (there was a US election that year) that contains a litany of anti-Reagan/Bush bile ("I know this is vitriol, no solution, spleen-venting, but I feel better for having screamed, don't you?"). The following month Bill Clinton was elected to office. Both Mills and Stipe have gone on record as hating this one (Mills: "I didn't like it the day we did it." Stipe: "We should have left it off the record"). Scott Litt plays clavinet and harmonica, and makes it sound like a brass section.

STAR ME KITTEN

R.E.M. turn their attention to sex (to which they would return for most of 'Monster'). Peter Buck: "It's a real perverse love song, demented. It's an endearing term. It's not about cats." Just as well, since at one point Stipe gets audibly more direct, clearly singing "Fuck me, kitten" (which was the song's original title, until Warners objected; the new name echoes The Rolling Stones having to change 'Starfucker' to 'Star Star'). Smoochy and seductive.

MAN ON THE MOON

Gentle but infectious, this one had 'hit' written all over it. Buck called it "a goofy look at heaven". The song is addressed to the late Andy Kaufman, a radical stand-up comic best known outside of the USA for his role as Latke in the TV series *Taxi*. Kaufman often featured an Elvis impression in his act, hence Michael Stipe's own (credible) Elvis impression here. Throughout the Third World, there are many who seriously believe the Apollo missions were all faked in Hollywood.

Robyn Hitchcock: "The first two verses of 'Man In The Moon' were written by Bill – you can tell by the weird way the guitar works against the voice that it's not what a conventional songwriter would have done – and Peter wrote the middle eight."

Michael: "That was kind of a 'vomit song'. But it took five months of working up to it. That song was written and recorded on the day that it was delivered to the record company. Although it *was* kind of a 40-hour day."

NIGHTSWIMMING

Written pre-'Green', apparently. A gentle ode to the joys of nude swimming, with wonderfully restrained orchestration. Mike Mills: "It's something we used to do back in Athens.

Twenty or thirty of us would go skinnydipping at two in the morning – you know, build a fire and get naked. There was a very real possibility of the sheriff coming up. We were drinking and doing who knows what, and we could have gone to jail. Whereas now, no one does it any more, except once in a while we take a friend up there to show them. And even if you do go to swim, it's still not like it used to be, because no one knows about it, and there's really no chance of anyone coming down and bothering you."

Peter Buck also remembered those days fondly: "We used to go swimming naked. It would be summertime, it would be 100 degrees, there'd be like 100 of us... We were all younger, it was pre-AIDS, so no one had this fear of sex. You'd assume what would happen and it did." But Buck's comment did seem to lend weight to those who saw in the line "fear of getting caught" a reference to AIDS, rather than just the thrill of illicit nudity. But – I'd say – it *is* possible to mourn the loss of innocence that comes simply through age-ing *without* dragging AIDS into it.

FIND THE RIVER

Another song seemingly about mourning, yet affirming life. The ocean is often used by Sufi mystics as a metaphor for God. Asked by *Q*'s Adrian Deevoy whether his songs could make him cry, Michael Stipe replied: "Sometimes. 'Find The River' to me has a lot of emotional baggage. It doesn't have that much to do with anything that would make sense to anyone else but me particularly. I know the place I wrote it. I know the connections I had with it when I wrote it. I know connections that came afterwards, people that died. So, yes, I can sing that song, but we've tried and tried to work it into some form which will translate live and for whatever reason we can't seem to play it. It's like a curse ... But I do love that song. Mike and I, when we wrote it, would drive around Miami in a convertible at three in the morning, and sing along to it. No words, just singing, both of us doing these climbing harmonics. It was so much fun to... cure yourself in that way."

MONSTER

R.E.M.

MONSTER

RELEASED SEPTEMBER 1994. CURRENT ISSUE: WARNER BROTHERS 9362-45740-2

In 1994, Peter Buck admitted that the last two R.E.M. albums had been "so lavishly adorned that we felt we had stretched that to the limit. 'Automatic' is my favourite R.E.M. album, but we can't make something like that again."

They both wanted and needed something very different: a rock album they could play live. Though much of the material from 'Out Of Time' and 'Automatic' could easily be played in concert, they felt the need of some crowd-pleasing anthemic stuff, and they didn't want to tour with a 'greatest hits' show. They needed some *new* loud songs. "It had to sound like four guys just playing in a room again," Peter said later.

Peter Buck, 1994: "We just said, 'okay, everyone write rock 'n' roll songs' – and it was great because we all met and we each had, like, ten songs – Bill, Mike and I. And then Michael had a bunch of lyrics and we put down about 24. We'd do about four a day, without even rehearsing them, just put them down and do them. So ideally, I'd like to do a really long record next time, maybe 18-20 songs. And make it noisy – I'm ready for that. We are a rock 'n' roll band and it just feels kind of logical to turn the amps up and get the drum kit out and bash away..."

Which they did. Recording began in Acapulco, Mexico in October 1993. Recording continued through early 1994 at Kingsway Studio in New Orleans, Crossover Soundstage in Atlanta, Criteria Recording in Miami and Oceanway Recording in L.A.. Recording concluded in L.A. in July 1994. That Spring, Peter Buck had become the father of twin girls.

They defined the results in different ways. To Bill Berry, this was primarily a guitar album: "Because there were so many layers and embellishments on the last two records, we wanted to limit the amount of overdubs on this one as much as possible. When you do that, of course, you're left with very few elements, so it makes sense to select one of those sounds and whack it out a bit. So, it was vocals and guitar that we'd isolate and think, 'What can we do to this sound that already exists on tape, to make the track more special, without actually adding more information?' So we got creative with the amps. We used a Marshall for the first time and some digital delay and tremolo that was built into it. We

didn't set out to make a wild guitar record, it just turned out that way."

And to Stipe, it was all about sex: "'Monster' is our punk rock album. Very in your face. And very sexy: most of the songs are about sex and relationships." Though when Michael went so far as to describe his penis as "a marvellous specimen" and himself as "an equal opportunity letch" (which most people took as an admission of bi-sexuality), it seemed totally out of character. Had he re-invented himself once again? "That was just a line I fed the media," he admitted later. "It was something for them to bounce off a little bit, to give them an idea." Then again, maybe he regrets being so candid.

But – in art, anyway – where there's sex, there's usually death as well, to complete the circle. Stipe later admitted that 'Monster' "was difficult to record because it wasn't just writing about death, it was experiencing it first hand. It's been a rough year for me and for the whole band in terms of that kind of thing, just 'life' things. We accept them and there's no real controlling them or anything like that. That stuff really gives you a perspective that you don't have prior to that."

R.E.M. had lost good friends: among them River Phoenix (to whom the album is dedicated) and Nirvana's Kurt Cobain (whose suicide inspired 'Let Me In'). Michael Stipe: "'Automatic For The People' got across that kind of idea of passage and mortality and that for me was quite a hurdle, speaking as a writer. I didn't want to go back to that with this record. We wound up doing 'Let Me In' on the record because it was just so much a part of the making of 'Monster'. I wrote the song for myself, basically, but it really fitted on the album so we stuck it in there anyway. But that aside, I think we all felt with 'Automatic...' that we had done as good a job as we possibly could do with a quiet kind of undertow music. We wanted to do something a lot more kinda fucked up and one-dimensional and right in front of you."

Mike Mills put it more bluntly : "We've done the crystal clear and clear thing. It was time to muddy it back up."

Once again, they had co-produced the album with Scott Litt. Mike Mills called him "the arbiter of disagreements. We turn to him when the four of us are so bound up in what we're doing that we can't see clearly. He's also a great engineer." Stipe was similarly complimentary: "The reason we've worked with him on five records is that he knows when to stand back and let things happen, and when to step in and offer advice. A lot of producers are either one or the other."

'Monster' may have been a great title for a rock guitar album, but the image had also surfaced several times before. "When the world is a monster," Stipe had sung on 'Can't Get There From Here', while the subtitle of their *Succumbs* video compilation reads: "The myth. The monster. The video."

With the album done, they looked forward to touring once again, despite the fact that they were five years older now. But as Peter told *Melody Maker*: "There's no reason why we can't do this for a long time. It's not as if our image or career is predicated on great youth or fashion. I mean, look at me. I'm an adult. I dress like this. I'm never gonna be in *GQ*. 'Automatic For The People' could very well have been written and recorded by 50-year-olds. There's no reason why we can't continue to do it. It just depends on how we look at ourselves. I can't imagine doing the same tour when I'm fifty. But Leonard Cohen

tours, and he's sixty."

As to their musical future, Buck had once told *Pulse!* magazine: "Every time you make a record, you think, why am I doing this? When we get to the point where we don't have anything to say to each other musically, you couldn't pay me to do it. If we start making bad records, I'll quit. But I'm still learning things. We do what we do. Eventually there'll be a time when we're not needed in the scheme of things. I'd like to think we'll figure it out before everyone else does."

WHAT'S THE FREQUENCY, KENNETH?

They've got a fuzzbox, and they're going to use it. And a wah-wah pedal! Strident guitar kicks off a very strange pop song. The title was a phrase allegedly uttered by gangsters who mugged American newscaster Dan Rather. Decades on from the last words of Dutch Schultz, it's nice to know that gangsters are still spouting Illuminati gibberish.

Scott Litt: "It was the song that was ready earliest. It was the one that they knew the best, and it was also the one where Michael had all his stuff done on. It was my idea to start with that and set a certain tone for the record. We got it really quickly. Then, unfortunately, Mike got appendicitis, and we had to stop for a week to ten days. In fact, a lot of the overdubs that are done on that song, the backwards guitar solos and stuff like that – we had a certain tape machine that featured a backwards recording function, and it was just kind of me playing around with it that led to doing certain stuff backwards because Mike was getting ready to get his appendix out and we were killing time."

CRUSH WITH EYELINER

Glam rock lives! Features backing vocals by Thurston Moore of Sonic Youth, and an adenoidal lead vocal from Michael. According to him this was inspired by The New York Dolls ("They also knew how to exaggerate a song, to make it sound really sleazy and over the top"), and the reference to "Frankenstein" is thus to the Dolls' song of that name. To these ears, there are also echoes of Lou Reed and Bowie. Live, Stipe apparently performs a mock striptease during this one (big deal. He's

been disrobing on stage for years), which fits with its aura of romantic lust ("won't you be my Valentine?"). Kurt Cobain's widow Courtney Love told *Rolling Stone* the song was about her – something Stipe later laughed off as a private joke between the two of them. "She's got a very arcane and dry sense of humour like I have, and often that does not translate well to press."

KING OF COMEDY

This sounds like *Low* -era Bowie (no bad thing), with the guitar buzzing like a synthesiser on heat. Lyrically, a self-mocking recipe for success. Stipe has said that he was consciously being playful here "with the image people have of me. Hopefully it's a shared joke." It should also be noted that there is a film with this title, Martin Scorcese's black comedy about fans and fanatics.

Scott Litt: "That started with kind of a riff and we built it up from there. That was done while we were mixing." Sally Dworski is on backing vocals.

I DON'T SLEEP, I DREAM

This starts like Cream's 'N.S.U.', then turns into a slow, bluesy lament. Stipe has introduced this one live as being his "second favourite song". Also as his "all-time favourite." He seems to say that kind of thing a lot.

Michael Stipe: "That song's nothing if it's not some sonic version of the dream state. At the end of the song it's like somebody dropped a huge book at the end of your bed while you're sleeping – BANG! – and you're out of it."

Peter Buck: "Michael's just really good at what he does. We write melodies for the songs, sometimes he'll use them, sometimes he doesn't, he'll just find something in there. 'I Don't Sleep, I Dream' is a perfect example – that was just a jam, a drumbeat and one chord. I figured he'd come up with something very amorphous for it, and I was really shocked that he had this really concise, melodic thing over the top that totally changed the song. He doesn't come up with stuff that I dislike."

STAR 69

Manically fast-paced rocker, the words coming so fast they blur (the delay/echo doesn't make them any clearer). The "Star" in the title is presumably referring back to 'Star Me Kitten' (i.e. "fuck"); "69" refers either to the year, or to oral sex.

STRANGE CURRENCIES

Slow, painfully honest romantic ballad that wouldn't have sounded out of place on 'Automatic'. The 'strings' sound electronic (actually, they sound like a Mellotron – a much underrated instrument).

TONGUE

Slow soulful ballad, with Michael singing in a falsetto, which has a real Memphis Soul feel to it, complete with Booker T-style organ.

Bill Berry: "We grew up in the South, soul was what was going on. 'Tongue' started out as a weird drum track that we recorded at a place in New Orleans where they have these wild drums, like Indian drums turned sideways. I started playing this beat and Scott rolled the tape. That's another example of how a song comes out of something completely uncalculated. Mike put on this big baseball-park organ, and then Michael decided to sing falsetto on it. I don't think he wanted to sound like Al Green or Smokey, but it does have that feel."

Michael Stipe: "I was trying to think how it would be if Tori Amos wrote a Prince cover song." Fair enough, since it's supposedly about cunnilingus. Then again, Stipe – who has since collaborated with Amos – may just have had his tongue in his cheek.

BANG AND BLAME

Sex, lies and paranoia: this starts off sounding like The Specials' 'Ghost Town', all menace and atmosphere, before suddenly going anthemic. The song itself seems to be about sexual hypocrisy, promiscuity and double standards. Backing vocals by: "Ane, Lynda, Lou and Rain", plus Sally Dworski.

I TOOK YOUR NAME

A paranoid rocker, with Michael sounding like Mick Jagger trying to be Dr. John, and Mike

Mills supplying suitably Stones-like backing vocals. This was the first of these songs to be written, according to Stipe. Written by Bill Berry (according to Scott Litt) late one night in his home studio. Engineer Mark Howard: "The vocal we recorded for 'I Took Your Name' was Michael singing on his back from a couch. I didn't know you could record vocals that way."

LET ME IN

A song of farewell "for, and about, Kurt." Cobain, that is, who had committed suicide in 1994. Stipe and Cobain had become friends some time before, and had planned to collaborate musically in the future. Cobain had even heard early demos of 'Monster'. Stipe called Cobain's death "a profound loss", later commenting that "Kurt's death was just a horrible mistake... a stupid mistake. There was a difference in him before his death – he had made a very vast change as a person, for the richer – which made his death much more of a shock." He told Musician magazine: "I had been talking to him at home up until his death, up until he disappeared. And so his death in some ways was not as much a shock to us as to everyone else. We knew he had been missing for seven days, and we knew a phone call would be coming at some point and we were hoping it would be a good one. And it wasn't."

Scott Litt: "'Let Me In' was another one that was written completely in the studio after we found out that Kurt died. Mike had that guitar riff and we put it down, and then put it on a Walkman for Michael. He was driving around in his car and he put the tape in there that just had the guitar and he sang along with it and taped it on a Walkman that was sitting on the front seat. That came very close to being on the record. He ended up re-singing it in the studio. But it almost was this Walkman tape that Michael made, because it was just so powerful. We were making this hard rock record, and then when we found out about Kurt it just devastated everybody, and all of a sudden this song came to be which really didn't fit in with the rest of the tone of the record. But it was important to the band and important to me and obviously important to Michael to get that on the record." The results are suitably gothic, despite the brashness of the guitar. You could imagine Nico singing this.

CIRCUS ENVY

Strange little rocker, with yet more guitar fuzz and featuring a return to animal imagery, with lyrics about circuses and jealousy. Did Michael want to be Corky the Circus Boy? Too bad, Michael Dolenz got there first. Sounds like he's singing through a megaphone again, or else he's suffering from the "pepper in my coffee".

YOU

The guitar here sounds like Richard Thompson circa 'Pour Down Like Silver'. Another seduction number, but a lot more desperate-sounding than 'Kitten' – this is about *real* obsession, one feels. It's bloody *epic*.

Scott Litt: "'You' was finished at the very end. It was the last to have lyrics and have a melody. That was done in the final mixing of the record." Fittingly, the record ends with feedback.

R.E.M.

eponymous

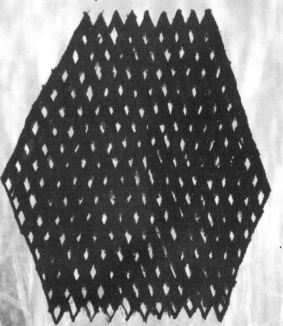

EPONYMOUS

RELEASED OCTOBER 1988. CURRENT ISSUE: IRS DMIRG 1038

Radio Free Europe/Gardening At Night/Talk About The Passion/So. Central Rain/(Don't Go Back To) Rockville/Can't Get There From Here/Driver 8/Romance (Night Garden)/Fall On Me/The One I Love/Finest Worksong/It's The End Of The World As We Know It (And I Feel Fine).

Released after the group had left IRS for Warners (its release came less than a month before that of 'Green'), though relations between the band and IRS were still good, according to Jay Boberg: "There was no vindictiveness." But with R.E.M. riding so high, it was inevitable that IRS would want to capitalise on their assets.

R.E.M. co-operated with the project, doubtless assuming that since IRS would go ahead with or without them, they might as well grin and bear it and produce something *they* were happy with. They provided sleeve notes, while Michael oversaw the design of the sleeve. The package included Michael's high school graduation photograph (a masterpiece of Seventies' iconography) superimposed with the words: "they airbrushed my face." Sleeve designer Geoff Gans relates that, "Originally it was going to have everybody's childhood photos on it, but no one else was willing to do it."

Subtitled 'File Under Grain' (to draw attention to famine – "hunger song" 'Talk About The Passion' was released as a single at the time), the album is basically a satisfactory 'hits' retrospective with a few hard-to-get goodies thrown in to tempt completists. These are:

RADIO FREE EUROPE

Credited as the original single version, released on Jonny Hibbert's Hib-Tone Records (Hib-Tone HT 0001) in July 1981.

Only about seven thousand copies were pressed (and have since become lucrative collectors' items). Some listeners believe this to be *another* Mitch Easter mix, but that might just be the difference between a badly-pressed single (which some of them were) and a cleaned-up CD. "Mike and Jefferson think this crushes the other one like a grape," say the sleeve notes. I disagree, but it does have a kind of naïve charm, with Bill drumming like a madman.

Jonny Hibbert described it as "a record that was just full of energy, that made people want to dance, that was kind of fun and kind of mysterious all at once. It had an innocence, yet a slightly sardonic angle to it too, which to me is almost the quintessential American pop single."

Whether it's about college radio, pirate radio or American propaganda station broadcasting to Eastern Bloc countries is anybody's bet, but it was a shrewd commercial choice for a début – songs about the radio are almost guaranteed to get airplay. And it did, if only on college stations. Also got voted 'Single Of The Year' by the critics of New York's *Village Voice*. Mind you, as Jefferson Holt pointed out to *Rolling Stone* in 1987: "The thing is, the great

reviews and the Top Ten lists didn't change the fact that we were in a '75 Dodge Tradesman lugging all our gear ourselves and still showing up and playing to eight or nine people."

GARDENING AT NIGHT

The original vocal take, which was replaced by another for the finished 'Chronic Town' release. This one is less mannered, and sounds more innocent, more like a demo. "Written on a mattress in the front yard," say the sleeve notes.

ROMANCE (NIGHT GARDEN)

This song dates back to 1981 and was one of several songs written to fill out their set in time for their first New York gig. Recorded for 'Murmur', but never released – pleasantly poppy, it sounds like it would have fitted better on 'Reckoning'. (Peter: "That was Mitch's favourite song of ours for a while. On all our albums, he would say, 'God, I really wish you guys would do 'Romance'"). This version was done in 1986 for the soundtrack of the movie *Made In Heaven*. Produced by Scott Litt and R.E.M. (their first session together).

FINEST WORKSONG

"Mutual drum horn mix," reads the subtitle. Horns had been added for the "lengthy club mix" B-side of the single release (see 'Document'); "this is the 'should-have-been' horn mix had instinct prevailed at the time," say the sleeve notes. It's certainly less self-indulgent (not difficult), but I still prefer the album version.

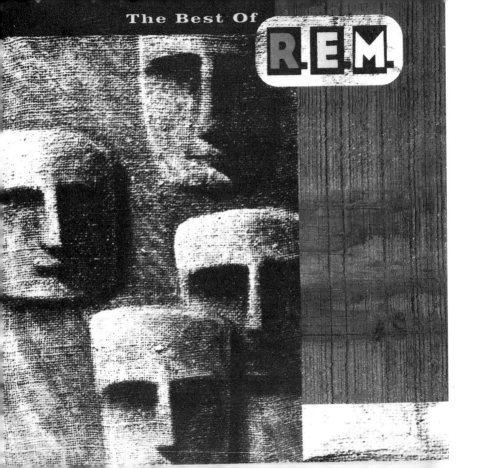

The Best Of R.E.M.

THE BEST OF R.E.M.

RELEASED SEPTEMBER 1991. CURRENT ISSUE: IRS MIRH 1

Carnival Of Sorts/Radio Free Europe/Perfect Circle/Talk About The Passion/So. Central Rain/Pretty Persuasion/Green Grow The Rushes/Can't Get There From Here/Fall On Me/I Believe/Cuyahoga/The One I Love/Finest Worksong/It's The End Of The World As We Know It (And I Feel Fine).

Released solely as a result of IRS changing its UK distribution and wanting to rake in a few extra pennies. Holt and Downs claim the group were not consulted about the content or packaging; IRS claim they were. That's showbiz...

In 1992, Peter Buck expressed his dissatisfaction with IRS re-releasing the group's back catalogue with extra tracks (as the 'IRS Years' series): "It must be a coincidence, but every time we put something out, they re-release something. I look at extra tracks they have on the record, and I'm sure some guy at the company taped them off the TV with his VCR, because they're mono, and not very good quality. I wonder if this year they're going to use our ad campaign. They've done it before."

THE AUTOMATIC BOX

RELEASED 1993. CURRENT ISSUE: WARNERS 9362-41268-2

A German import: a boxed set of four CD's, each containing only four or five tracks, which compiles various B-sides from 'Green' to 'Automatic For The People'. No sleeve notes, minimal track information given. Not available in the US.

Disc 1 – Vocal Tracks:

IT'S A FREE WORLD BABY

An 'Out Of Time' out-take (it nearly made it to the finished album), released as a B-side to 'Drive'. "I can't feel anything," complains Michael, in what seems to be a weary (too tired to be bitter) carp about (or to) a lover.

FRETLESS

Another 'Out Of Time' out-take, and more moaning about sex – this time an emotional/sexual triangle that's coming to an end – featuring Kate Pierson on backing vocals. This first surfaced on the soundtrack of the Wim Wenders movie, *Until The End Of The World* (Stipe has often cited Wenders' *Wings Of Desire* as one of his favourite films). Buck: "We had a couple of things we'd finished that were good, but the tempo or key or theme of the song didn't fit in on the record, and that was one of them." He's also called it "the worst song we wrote this whole year." Some of the lyrics come from an (abandoned) song titled 'Here I Am Again'. Also released as a B-side to 'The Sidewinder Sleeps Tonight'.

CHANCE

Spoken/intoned vocal, set against a Parisian accordion sound and techno beat. Mournful, impressionistic diary of a relationship that's occasionally funny ("You left, I worried"), which ends when Michael (?) accurately points out that it's getting tedious. Presumably a B-side, though I couldn't track down which single. Subtitled "Dub".

STAR ME KITTEN

Demo version, first released as a B-side to 'Everybody Hurts'. A lot earthier than the album version, and not just because they're plainly singing "fuck me, kitten" throughout. They're practically *growling* it. "Do you like it?" asks Michael at the end.

Disc 2 – Instrumental Tracks (All 'Automatic' out takes):

WINGED MAMMAL THEME

'Automatic...' out take, first released as a B-side to 'Drive'. Jazzy electric piano, sweeping strings, plus the singer intoning one word ("Batman") in the background (which explains the title). An odd one.

ORGAN SONG

Aimless Gothic churchy organ meandering. Recorded in Minneapolis in November 1991. B-side of 'Sidewinder Sleeps Tonight'.

MANDOLIN STRUM

The mandolin is one of those rare instruments that sounds fab no matter what you do with it. This sounds like Mason Williams meeting Nick Drake, attempting to teach him a George Harrison song and failing. First released as a B-side to 'Drive'.

FRUITY ORGAN

Bouncily whimsical nonsensical pop, which sounds like they had fun doing it. First released as a B-side to 'Man In The Moon'.

NEW ORLEANS INSTRUMENTAL No. 2

Schmoozy schmalz that sounds like a Seventies' movie theme. Actually, it sounds like 'Suicide Is Painless' from *M.A.S.H.*. First released as a B-side to 'Man In The Moon'.

With all these instrumentals, you kind of wonder why they bothered.

Disc 3 – Cover Versions:

ARMS OF LOVE

An 'Automatic' out take. Cover of a song by ex-Soft Boy Robyn Hitchcock, and this version is simply wonderful. It may well make you want to check out Hitchcock's own work, much of which features Peter Buck guesting on guitar. First released as a B-side to 'Man In The Moon'.

DARK GLOBE

Strangely faithful version of Syd Barrett song. First released as a B-side to 'Orange Crush'. Stipe on, you crazy diamond.

THE LION SLEEPS TONIGHT

A.k.a. 'Wimoweh', as recorded by (among others) Miriam Makeba, The Tokens, Karl Denver and the terrible Tight Fit. There's also a fine version by Brian Eno, for those of you who like tracking down B-sides. An old favourite of R.E.M.'s – they'd recorded a demo way back in 1983 – recorded in Athens in November 1992, and they sound like they had a ball doing it. It's great fun to listen to, too. First released (appropriately enough) as a B-side to 'The Sidewinder Sleeps Tonight'.

FIRST WE TAKE MANHATTAN

Peter Buck described their version of this Leonard Cohen song as being: "Enormous drums and screeching guitars. It sounds like The Gang Of Four and Sonic Youth meet Neil Young." It also sounds doom-laden and Germanic. This first appeared on the Cohen-tribute album 'I'm Your Fan', of which Buck noted: "Barring one or two tracks on which I didn't like the performances, I was kind of amazed how well suited his songs are to being adapted to different areas, and how good the songs are." Also released as a B-side to 'Drive'.

Disc 4 — B-Sides:

GHOSTRIDER

Cover version of a Suicide song that's full of punk clichés; Michael sounds suitably bored. First released as a B-side to 'Orange Crush'.

FUNTIME

Mannered cover version of the Iggy Pop song "recorded and mixed in four minutes at John Keane's studios, Athens," 1989. Presumably a B-side, but I couldn't track down the single.

MEMPHIS TRAIN BLUES

Short jazzy blues, dominated by mandolin, bass and train noises. First released as a B-side to 'Stand'.

POP SONG '89

Acoustic, folksy version. Not a good idea – it doesn't really translate well. First released as the B-side to 'Stand'.

EVERYBODY HURTS

Better than adequate live version, recorded at the 1993 MTV awards. First released as the B-side to 'Find The River'.

AND FINALLY...

There has yet to be an official Warners retrospective (it's just a matter of time), but 'The Automatic Box' is already out of date, as virtually every single since has had unreleased tracks on the B-side (most of them live versions – of variable quality and interest – of known songs). There are also several other cover versions released on 'tribute' albums, including Suzanne Vega's 'Tom's Diner', Roky Erikson's 'I Walked With A Zombie' and Richard Thompson's 'Wall Of Death' – plus a slew of material issued as Christmas singles, only available to fan club members. This material does not appear in this book, as much of it is hard or impossible to find; doubtless it will be compiled in album form at some date, and will then be reviewed in a future edition.

That there is plenty of material in the vaults is beyond doubt, as Buck admitted in 1993: "Our lawyer was real farsighted and had us recording shows 24-track when we first got our recording contract. So every tour we've done, there's probably five songs recorded... then of course all the stuff in the studio, which is on a computer, and all our video stuff which we own the rights to. We've got this little vault in Atlanta. It's kind of a daunting prospect to look at – hundreds and hundreds of hours of tapes.

"When we were getting off IRS, we were looking for one particular song that we wanted to use for a B-side, and it was the only thing we couldn't find. And none of us could remember how to play the song! I still think that's floating around somewhere, but it's the only thing we're missing as far as I can tell. That's when we got the computer and sent this poor guy looking for a song that was either called 'the new song' or 'the new song'. We have about fifty 'new songs' spread out over the space of ten years." And Buck has stated that R.E.M. probably know

over a thousand songs! Then again, he has been known to exaggerate ...

Hopefully, there's more than enough good archive material to justify an R.E.M. boxed set. If it's compiled with as much care as 'Dead Letter Office', I, for one, am ready for it.

In addition to their work as R.E.M., group members (the workaholic Buck in particular) have all sallied forth in various other guises down the years, as both producers and musicians, contributing to an ever-growing list of records by other artists. This, despite their own gruelling recording and touring schedules – these guys really are gluttons for punishment! How you feel about these records probably depends on how you feel about the artist in question (some I like, some I don't), but since none of them are actually R.E.M. records as such, I haven't covered them here. Anyone interested in checking out these records is recommended to consult the discography in Tony Fletcher's *Remarks* and the appropriate section in Marcus Gray's *It Crawled From The South*.

VIDEOS

"**V**ideos suck," said Peter Buck in 1992, summing up his long-held views on the subject. Years before, he'd said: "I've never seen a video that made me like a song. Ours, I think, are half-dumb and half-intelligent. I give so little thought to it that I don't really care." Mike Mills echoed these sentiments in 1992: "Michael has the visual sense in this group. The rest of us just don't much give a shit."

Michael Stipe was indeed the mover and shaker behind all sleeve artwork, but even he had initially been reluctant to get involved in video. And video – ever since MTV had kicked into gear at the turn of the Eighties – has been deemed essential exposure territory by the music industry. But Stipe's views were to change, as he explained in 1991: "I've always taken a strong stand against lip-synching for its falseness. In the last year I've realised that – yes, lip-synching is fake, videos are fake, television is fake, film is fake, the experience of watching it is fake. Everything about it is not real. The realness involved is the emotion that comes through and the message that gets across. I think we pushed video as far as we could without lip-synching, so the natural step

for me was to try it, and if I'm good then it's an option. Based on the calls I got from the directors of 'Losing My Religion' and 'Shiny Happy People' – who thought my performances on film were electrifying – it makes me feel like, maybe I can get that thing across without actually having to tour every corner of the world."

And it's arguable that video was indeed what finally propelled R.E.M. into the mega-sales bracket. The 'Out Of Time' CS videos were given heavy airplay on MTV, and gained R.E.M. more exposure than a year of touring would have done (and they weren't touring at all at this point), with far less wear and tear on the system. And now that they've finally warmed to it a bit, they've been producing interesting and witty videos, though many still fall into the one-man-singing-three-guys-standing-about trap, which probably exacerbates Stipe's problems as a media focus.

Several compilation tapes are currently available :

SUCCUMBS
RELEASED 1987. CURRENT ISSUE: A&M
VIDEO/POLYGRAM VIDEO - 630 290 3

Radio Free Europe/So. Central Rain/Left of Reckoning/Can't Get There From Here/Driver 8/Life And How To Live It/'Feeling Gravity's Pull/Fall On Me
Introduced by Peter Buck and Jefferson Holt as being "a representative sampling of an outmoded artform" this collects all the early IRS videos. 'Left of Reckoning' features various songs from that album accompanied by film , shot by Athens art teacher Jim Herbert: moody, grainy footage of the group wandering about local sculptor Rubin Miller's whirligig garden, fooling around in a warehouse etc. It looks like The Monkees on acid, but less fun.

'Can't Get There From Here' guest stars manager Jefferson Holt, and proves that Michael Stipe dances exactly like Steve Martin. Throughout *all* these videos, the band look bored witless. Only 'Fall One Me' (directed by Michael) has any real impact – largely due to the lyrics flashing across the screen. As a collected package, this is pretty heavy going, and recommended only for diehard fans.

As Miles Copeland, head of IRS Records noted in 1994: "Occasionally, I wondered about those obscure videos they were making. But they were the only act, apart from Sting, that I can think of that actually said, 'We'll pay the price – if it isn't a hit then it isn't a hit, and if it is a hit, great.' And they meant it. They had videos that they literally weren't in that weren't very good, in my view. I just didn't think we were going to see a lot of action out of those videos, and I was right – we didn't. Still don't. I think if they had made a few concessions we would have had success earlier."

ture the band peripherally or not at all. Sometimes this seems pointless artiness, sometimes – as with 'Talk About The Passion', which contrasts images of poverty and homelessness with those of military spending – it works. 'Pop Song '89' features Michael Stipe cavorting topless with three topless female go-go dancers (supposedly friends), and is actually pretty funny. When MTV demanded that the girls' nipples be censored (to protect the youth of America), R.E.M. promptly censored them all, including Michael's (Michael: "We took the view that a nipple was a nipple, so we got rid of them all.") A patchy collection, but all in all a lot more watchable than *Succumbs*.

POP SCREEN

RELEASED 1990. CURRENT ISSUE: WARNER
MUSIC VISION - 7599-38156-3

The One I Love/It's The End Of The World As We Know It (And I Feel Fine)/Finest Worksong/Talk About The Passion/Orange Crush/Stand/Turn You Inside-Out/Pop Song '89/Get Up
More promotional videos, many of which fea-

TOURFILM

RELEASED 1990. CURRENT ISSUE: WARNER
MUSIC VISION - 7599-38184-3

Stand/The One I Love/These Days/Turn You Inside Out/World Leader Pretend/Feeling Gravity's Pull/I Believe/I Remember California/Get Up/It's The End Of The World As We Know It (And I Feel Fine)/Pop Song

'89/Fall On Me/You Are The Everything/Begin The Begin/King Of Birds/Finest Worksong/Perfect Circle

Produced by Jim McKay with Michael Stipe. "In the first week of November 1989 we rolled tape and shot film at a number of shows... with a wild and unforgettable decade of touring behind us." These words close *Tourfilm*, and pretty much explain what it is: an atmospheric record/souvenir of the 'Green' shows. Eager to please their new major label, R.E.M. had set out on a massive worldwide tour, most of which comprised stadium gigs. Their line-up was augmented for this tour by Peter Holsapple on keyboards. Holsapple was the former guitarist and songwriter with The dB's, who had supported R.E.M. on the 'Document' tour, and he had also been their (solo) opening act way back in 1982.

But the stadium experience had not been a good one, as Bill Berry later summed up: "Halfway through the tour we were so burned out by it that we were just on stage going through the motions. We really felt we were robbing the audience of what they deserve. We were playing in arenas a little larger than we were comfortable with and the whole thing was pretty depressing." They wouldn't tour again until 1995 and 'Monster'.

The strain doesn't show here, though. The film itself might not be the greatest concert film ever (it owes more than a little to Talking Heads' *Stop Making Sense*) but it still features some imaginative intercutting between concerts, and thanks to the use of four camera people (and the direction of Declan Quinn), it's seldom dull visually or aurally. This is R.E.M. doing what they do very well indeed, and on great form.

And Michael Stipe is a riveting performer, as fond of silly dancing as he is of silly haircuts. "He dresses like a five-year-old," a friend of mine once observed, and here he's decked out in a baggy suit that compounds the comparisons with David Byrne (it was made by the same tailor that made Byrne's *Stop Making Sense* suit – but where Byrne just looked eccentric, Michael does indeed look like a kid who's stolen his dad's clothes). He uses the bare minimum of props (a megaphone, a music stand), and the stage set itself is almost bare (though with an imaginative use of lighting and back projected films).

Michael Stipe, 1988: "I realised last year that people were paying $16.50 to see something. There's some songs I can't sing unless I move – I literally can't hit the notes unless I'm moving. I always paint my eyebrows. I'm big on eyebrows. It's vaudeville, it's Dickensian, it's a comedy of errors, it's entertainment."

He also uses ridiculously heavy eyeliner, which makes him look at times like a bizarre clown/mime, at others like a Holocaust victim, at others like the young Elvis Presley. "Raccoon eyes," he calls them. He's totally compelling.

Odd moments stick in the brain: Stipe singing 'You Are The Everything' with his back to the audience (hinting, perhaps, that the song is a prayer); Stipe introducing both 'Begin The Begin' and 'Finest Worksong' with the identical refrain: "this is a song of personal and political activism, and it's written especially for you"; a great version of 'King Of Birds', with Peter's slide guitar morphing into sitarry psychedelia... It all winds up with a raucous version of the Velvets' 'Afterhours' at the closing show in Atlanta, Stipe singing joyously: "If we close the door, I'll never have to see the world again."

And, for a while, they closed the door.

After this, they *needed* some seclusion. Essential viewing (there was a point while writing this book when I'd rather have jabbed needles in my eye than listen to another R.E.M. song; watching this renewed my enthusiasm).

THIS FILM
IS ON
RELEASED 1991. CURRENT ISSUE: WARNER MUSIC VISION · 7599 38254-3

Losing My Religion/Shiny Happy People/Near Wild Heaven/Radio Song/Love Is All Around/Losing My Religion (Acoustic)/Low/Belong/Half A World Away/Country Feedback

Mainly 'Out Of Time' promotional videos, plus two live TV clips: an acoustic version of 'Losing My Religion' from BBC TV's *The Late Show*, plus a cover of the old Troggs' song 'Love Is All Around' from the band's 1991 MTV *Unplugged*, again acoustic. In fact, it's practically folk-rock, with Mike on lead vocals, great mandolin from Peter and a sublime vocal harmony from Michael.

The song – written by The Troggs' Reg Presley – was later covered by Wet Wet Wet, as part of the soundtrack to the movie *Four Weddings & A Funeral*. It went on to sell megaunits, and made a surprised Reg Presley suddenly rich. Why that version was chosen over R.E.M.'s remains one of life's incomprehensible mysteries (Richard Curtis, you should know better). There was talk around this time of R.E.M. doing an EP of Troggs' songs, which sadly never happened ("I think it'd be a great idea," said Buck, but he was evidently unable to convince the others). Instead Mills, Buck, Berry and Holsapple contributed to The Troggs' 1992 album 'Athens Andover', which is recommended for diehards only.

As to *Unplugged*, it's intimate and laid back, the group playing while sat on stools (Bill on congas). It's unlikely to see a commercial release, so pester MTV to repeat it in your area.

The most notable promotional videos here are the ones for 'Losing My Religion', which owes a lot to both Wim Wenders and Derek Jarman (its use of homoerotic imagery combined with religious imagery meant it was banned in Ireland; actually, it features images from several religions, but only the Catholics complained), and 'Shiny Happy People', which is a lot of fun. Kate Pierson looks unbelievably sexy, Michael looks like someone on their way to their first day at kindergarten, and everyone else (except Peter Buck) really looks like they're enjoying themselves. Worth buying for these alone.

Promotional videos aside, there are numerous other film and TV footage in the R.E.M. vaults, dating back to their appearance on the David Letterman show in 1983. Hopefully at some point these will be compiled into a documentary.

Index

7 CHINESE BROTHERS 13

9-9 ....8, 9

1,000,000 43

AGES OF YOU 38

ALL THE RIGHT FRIENDS 43

ARMS OF LOVE 101

AUCTIONEER (ANOTHER ENGINE) 26

BANDWAGON 27, 39

BANG AND BLAME 89

BEGIN THE BEGIN 31

BELONG...70

BURNING DOWN 37

BURNING HELL 27, 38

CAMERA...16

CAN'T GET THERE FROM HERE 25

CARNIVAL OF SORTS (BOX CARS) 43

CATAPULT..8, 9

CHANCE...99

CHRONIC TOWN 40

CIRCUS ENVY 90

COUNTRY FEEDBACK 70

CRAZY 27, 37

CRUSH WITH EYELINER 87

CUYAHOGA...32

DARK GLOBE 101

DISTURBANCE AT THE HERON HOUSE 48, 52

(DON'T GO BACK TO) ROCKVILLE............16

DREAM (ALL I HAVE TO DO) 35

DRIVE 76

DRIVER 8 ....23, 27

ENDGAME 69

EVERYBODY HURTS 77, 102

EXHUMING MCCARTHY 47

FALL ON ME 32

FEELING GRAVITYS PULL 23

FEMME FATALE 39

FIND THE RIVER 79

FINEST WORKSONG 47, 51, 52, 95

FIREPLACE 49

FIRST WE TAKE MANHATTAN 101

FLOWERS OF GUATEMALA, THE 33

FRETLESS 99

FRUITY ORGAN 100

FUNTIME 102

GARDENING AT NIGHT 9, 41, 43, 94

GET UP 57

GHOSTRIDER.......................................102

GOOD ADVICES.....................................26

GREEN GROW THE RUSHES 25
HAIRSHIRT 60
HALF A WORLD AWAY 70
HARBORCOAT 13
HYENA 32
I BELIEVE 33
I DON'T SLEEP, I DREAM 88
I REMEMBER CALIFORNIA 61
I TOOK YOUR NAME 89
IGNORELAND 78
IT'S A FREE WORLD BABY 99
IT'S THE END OF THE WORLD AS WE KNOW IT
(AND I FEEL FINE) 48
JUST A TOUCH 33, 35
KING OF BIRDS 50
KING OF COMEDY 87
KING OF THE ROAD 39
KOHOUTEK 26
LAST DATE 51
LAUGHING 7
LET ME IN..89
LETTER NEVER SENT 15
LIFE AND HOW TO LIVE IT 24
LIGHTNIN' HOPKINS 50
LION SLEEPS TONIGHT, THE..........................101
LITTLE AMERICA...16
LOSING MY RELIGION....................................68

LOW 68
MAN ON THE MOON 79
MANDOLIN STRUM.......................................100
MAPS AND LEGENDS 23, 27
ME IN HONEY 71
MEMPHIS TRAIN BLUES................................102
MONTY GOT A RAW DEAL 78
MOON RIVER 17
MORAL KIOSK 7
NEAR WILD HEAVEN 69
NEW ORLEANS INSTRUMENTAL NO.1 78
NEW ORLEANS INSTRUMENTAL NO.2 100
NIGHTSWIMMING..79
ODDFELLOWS LOCAL 151 50
OLD MAN KENSEY 25
ONE I LOVE, THE 49, 51
ORANGE CRUSH 60
ORGAN SONG..100
PALE BLUE EYES 38
PERFECT CIRCLE 7
PILGRIMAGE 6
POP SONG 89 ....57, 102
PRETTY PERSUASION 15, 17
RADIO FREE EUROPE 5, 93
RADIO SONG 67
ROMANCE (NIGHT GARDEN) 94
ROTARY TEN 35, 39

SECOND GUESSING 15

SHAKING THROUGH 8

SHINY HAPPY PEOPLE....................................69

SIDEWINDER SLEEPS TONIGHT, THE 77

SITTING STILL 8

SO. CENTRAL RAIN..15

STAND 58

STAR 69 88

STAR ME KITTEN 79, 100

STRANGE 48

STRANGE CURRENCIES 88

STUMBLE 43

SUPERMAN..34

SWAN SWAN H 34, 35

SWEETNESS FOLLOWS 78

TALK ABOUT THE PASSION...............................7

TEXARKANA...70

THERE SHE GOES AGAIN 9, 37

THESE DAYS 32

TIGHTEN UP 17

TIME AFTER TIME (ANNELISE) 15, 51

TIRED OF SINGING TROUBLE 35

TONGUE...88

TOYS IN THE ATTIC 35, 38

TRY NOT TO BREATHE 77

TURN YOU INSIDE OUT 60

UNDERNEATH THE BUNKER 33

(UNTITLED)/ELEVENTH UNTITLED SONG, THE 61

VOICE OF HAROLD.......................................38

WALTER'S THEME...39

WE WALK 8

WELCOME TO THE OCCUPATION 47

WENDELL GEE...26

WEST OF THE FIELDS 9

WHAT IF WE GIVE IT AWAY............................33

WHAT'S THE FREQUENCY, KENNETH?.............. 86

WHITE TORNADO 17, 38

WINDOUT...16, 38

WINGED MAMMAL THEME 100

WOLVES, LOWER...40

WORLD LEADER PRETEND 58

WRONG CHILD, THE......................................60

YOU 90

YOU ARE THE EVERYTHING................................58

3/96 (23872)